SPARK
NOTES

LIBRARY *of* GREAT AUTHORS

SPARK
NOTES

LIBRARY *of* GREAT AUTHORS

Albert Camus
Lewis Carroll
Fyodor Dostoevsky
Barbara Kingsolver
Gabriel García Márquez
Toni Morrison
Vladimir Nabokov
J.K. Rowling
J.R.R. Tolkien
Virginia Woolf

SPARK
NOTES

LIBRARY *of* GREAT AUTHORS

J.K. Rowling

Her Life and Works

Charles Lovett

EDITORIAL DIRECTOR Justin Kestler
EXECUTIVE EDITOR Ben Florman
SERIES EDITOR Emma Chastain

INTERIOR DESIGN Dan Williams

Produced by The Wonderland Press and published by SparkNotes

Spark Publishing
A Division of SparkNotes LLC
120 5th Avenue
New York, NY 10011

10 9 8 7 6 5 4 3 2 1

Please submit comments or questions, or report errors to *www.sparknotes.com/errors*.

Printed and bound in the United States of America

ISBN 1-58663-839-4

Cover photograph copyright © 2003 by Corbis, Inc.

Library of Congress Cataloging-in-Publication Data available on request

Contents

Contents

III.

{ Harry Potter and the Chamber of Secrets 61 }

Key Facts 63

Reading *Harry Potter and the Chamber of Secrets*. 71

IV.

{ Harry Potter and the Prisoner of Azkaban }
109

Contents

{ Topics In Depth }

SPARK NOTES

The
LIBRARY *of*
GREAT AUTHORS
series explores the
intimate connection between
writing and experience, shedding light
on the work of literature's most esteemed
authors by examining their lives. The
complete LIBRARY *of* GREAT AUTHORS brings
an excitingly diverse crowd to your bookshelf,
from Fyodor Dostoevsky to J.K. Rowling.

Each book in the LIBRARY *of* GREAT AUTHORS
features full-length analysis of the writer's
most famous works, including such novels as
*Crime and Punishment, Lolita, The Lord of
the Rings*, and *Mrs. Dalloway*. Whether you
are a reader craving deeper knowledge of
your favorite author, a student studying the
classics, or a new convert to a celebrated
novel, turn to the LIBRARY *of* GREAT AUTHORS
for thorough, fascinating, and insightful
coverage of literature's best writers.

LIBRARY *of* GREAT AUTHORS

J.K. Rowling

I

THE LIFE OF J.K. ROWLING

Joanne Kathleen Rowling was born in Chipping Sodbury, in western England, on July 31, 1965. As a little girl, she lived in Yate, near the port city of Bristol, with her parents and her little sister, **Diana**. Her father, **Peter Rowling**, was an engineer, and her mother, **Ann Rowling**, was a laboratory technician. Both of Rowling's parents loved books and exposed their children to great works of literature. From an early age, Rowling enjoyed telling stories to her sister.

"The first story I ever wrote down (when I was five or six) was about a rabbit called Rabbit," said Rowling. "He got the measles and was visited by his friends, including a giant bee called Miss Bee. And ever since Rabbit and Miss Bee, I have wanted to be a writer, though I rarely told anyone so. I was afraid they'd tell me I didn't have a hope."

Rowling's family moved twice during her early childhood, first to another Bristol suburb called Winterbourne and then to the country village of Tutshill, near the Welsh border. Rowling's parents, both raised in the noise and rush of London, had always wanted to raise their children in the country. Their home in Tutshill provided an idyllic environment for their two daughters to wander through safely.

Placed at a new school, Rowling quickly learned about classroom politics. "My new teacher, **Mrs. Morgan**, gave me an arithmetic test on the very first morning, and after a huge effort I managed to get zero out of ten—I had never done fractions before. So she sat me in the row of desks on her far right. It took me a few days to realize I was in the 'stupid' row. . . . By the end of the year, I had been promoted . . . but at a cost. Mrs. Morgan made me swap seats with my best friend, so that in one short walk across the room I became clever but unpopular."

At comprehensive school (the British equivalent of American high school) Rowling was, she has said, "quiet, freckly, short-sighted, and rubbish at sports." Rowling loved her English classes and especially enjoyed the novels of Jane Austen. During school, Rowling continued to write stories but rarely showed them to anyone. In her last year at Wyedean Comprehensive, Rowling was made Head Girl, a coveted position that involves representing one's school and directing prefects.

Rowling continued her education at Exeter University in southwest England, where she studied French and Classics. During her college career, she worked briefly as a teacher in Paris to earn class credit. After graduation, Rowling worked in the business world for several years, but she felt too disorganized to be effective. What she liked best about her office jobs was the opportunity they gave her to write stories using the office computer.

J. K. Rowling

After working for Amnesty International in London for two years, Rowling moved to Manchester with her boyfriend. She found work at the University of Manchester and later at the Manchester Chamber of Commerce. In 1990, when she was twenty-six, Rowling experienced a series of stressful events that changed her life. First, her mother, who had been diagnosed with multiple sclerosis in 1980, passed away. Rowling was subsequently robbed, and later lost her job as well. She decided to "give up on offices" and moved to Portugal to teach English as a foreign language.

> "I was taking a long train journey from Manchester to London in England and the idea for Harry just fell into my head. At that point it was essentially the idea for a boy who didn't know he was a wizard, and the wizard school he ended up going to. . . . The idea that we could have a child who escapes from the confines of the adult world and goes somewhere where he has power, both literally and metaphorically, really appealed to me."
>
> J.K. ROWLING

While working in Portugal, Rowling took notes, wrote outlines, and made sketches about a fictional character she had dreamed up, whom she called **Harry Potter**. Rowling, who had already written two adult novels she considered unworthy of publication, originally conceived of the Harry Potter books as a series for adults.

In 1991, Rowling met a Portuguese journalist named **Jorges Arantes**. The two were married in October 1992, and in July 1993, Rowling gave birth to a girl, **Jessica**. A few months after Jessica's birth, Rowling and Arantes divorced. Rowling moved with her infant daughter to Edinburgh, Scotland, where her sister Diana was living. Unable to find a job that would pay enough to cover living expenses and childcare costs, Rowling received public assistance for a time. She had written part of the first Harry Potter book in Portugal, and continued writing in Edinburgh, often writing in a café near her home, Jessica sleeping in a stroller next to her. Rowling wrote the novel in longhand and typed the final draft on a manual typewriter. In 1995, she completed *Harry Potter and the Philosopher's Stone*.

By the time she completed the novel, Rowling had secured employment as a French teacher. She sent the novel to an agent, **Christopher Little**, who showed it to several publishers, most of whom considered the book too long to appeal to children. In 1996, Bloomsbury Publishing in London agreed to publish the book.

They paid Rowling an advance of £2,500 ($3,300) and printed only 500 copies of her novel. However, the publishers soon realized that Harry had the potential for huge popularity. In 1997, Scholastic, a New York publisher, offered Rowling a $105,000 advance to publish the novel in America. The advance gave Rowling the financial stability to write full time without worrying about money. The novel was published in America under the title *Harry Potter and the Sorcerer's Stone*.

Eventually, *Harry Potter and the Sorcerer's Stone*, along with its successors, became an unprecedented publishing phenomenon, selling tens of millions of copies worldwide. The first four Harry Potter books in the planned seven-book series have earned critical acclaim, won numerous awards, and become the first children's books to

> "I didn't think it would do this well with anyone. I thought I was writing quite an obscure book that, if it ever got published, would maybe have a handful of devotees. . . . I never expected it to have broad appeal."
>
> **J.K. ROWLING**

top bestseller lists. Now an international celebrity in constant demand by journalists, talk show hosts, and fans, Rowling is still living a quiet life in Edinburgh and working on Harry's saga. She has expressed shock at Harry's incredible popularity, since she originally wrote the story for herself. She says she will always keep writing, even when she must leave Harry and Hogwarts behind.

J. K. Rowling

Rowling's Literary Context

Her Influences and Impact

The Harry Potter series can be read as fairy tales, satires, detective novels, and epic fantasies of good and evil. Perhaps the literary genre they best fit is the bildungsroman, or coming-of-age novel. The attributes of the bildungsroman, as enumerated by Marianne Hirsch in a 1979 article in *Genre*, include a focus on the "growth and development" of one character "within the context of a defined social order," and the quest for "meaningful existence within society." A bildungsroman includes, in addition to its protagonist, secondary characters such as educators, companions, and lovers. Novels in this genre are often didactic and concerned with the main character's developing sense of identity.

> "I am told that children have started to read [the Harry Potter books]. They are certainly popular with one of my grandchildren."
>
> QUEEN ELIZABETH II, ON MEETING J.K. ROWLING

The Harry Potter series belongs to a bildungsroman tradition reaching back to **Goethe** (1749–1832) and including such classic English novels as **Jane Austen**'s (1775–1817) *Emma* (1816) and **Charles Dickens**'s (1812–1870) *David Copperfield* (1850) and *Great Expectations* (1861). In American literature, the adolescent search for identity often includes a period of rebellion, as in the case of **Mark Twain**'s (1835–1910) *Huckleberry Finn* (1884) and of Holden Caulfield in **J.D. Salinger**'s (b. 1919) *The Catcher in the Rye* (1951). Harry's frequent disregard for school rules links him with this American twist on the bildungsroman.

Charles Dickens, a nineteenth-century novelist of staggering popularity, is perhaps the writer closest to Rowling in spirit, technique, and impact. Harry bears more than a passing resemblance to notable Dickensian orphans like David Copperfield and Oliver Twist—independent, brave boys who begin their fictional journeys in bad straits, ground down under the heel of cruel adults. Like Dickens, Rowling gives her characters colorful names that suggest their personalities. Draco Malfoy, Petunia Dursley, and Albus Dumbledore, Rowling creations, are the literary successors of Dickens characters such as Uriah Heep, Bumble, and Ebenezer Scrooge. Like Dickens, Rowling uses physical descriptions of characters to hint at their personalities. Like Dickens, Rowling includes narrative details that become increasingly significant as the stories progress. Finally, like Dickens, Rowling delivers her Harry Potter story in installments, a strategy

"Part of the secret of Rowling's success is her utter traditionalism. The Potter story is a fairy tale, plus a bildungsroman, plus a murder mystery, plus a cosmic war of good and evil, and there's almost no classic in any of those genres that doesn't reverberate between the lines of Harry's saga. . . . Rowling's books are chock-a-block with archetypes, and she doesn't just use them; she glories in them."

JOAN ACOCELLA, *THE NEW YORKER*

that works her fans into a frenzy of anticipation. Just as American Dickens fans waited at the New York pier for the ship that bore the latest installment of *The Old Curiosity Shop*, Potter fans gather in long lines outside bookstores, waiting for the release of the newest Harry Potter installment.

Critics and scholars often liken Rowling's work to the fiction of **J.R.R. Tolkien** (1892–1973), author of the fantasy series *The Lord of the Rings* (1954–1955), another popular collection of stories steeped in magic and fantasy, which is enjoying a resurgence thanks to its own well-received film adaptation.

Rowling's Potter series also recalls the stories of **Roald Dahl** (1916–1990), which include *James and the Giant Peach* (1961), *Charlie and the Chocolate Factory* (1964), *The Witches* (1983), and *Matilda* (1988). Dahl's stories, like Rowling's, feature magical child-protagonists coming of age and dealing with the cruelties and mysteries of adults.

II

HARRY POTTER AND THE SORCERER'S STONE

Key Facts

Genre: Children's fantasy novel, bildungsroman (coming-of-age novel); the first in a planned series of seven novels

Date of First Publication: 1997, England, as *Harry Potter and the Philosopher's Stone*; 1998, United States, as *Harry Potter and the Sorcerer's Stone*

Setting: Modern-day England. London and the Hogwarts School of Witchcraft and Wizardry

Narrator: Anonymous, third-person observer

Plot Overview: Harry Potter, who lives with his horrid aunt and uncle, discovers that he is a wizard and is accepted into the Hogwarts School of Witchcraft and Wizardry. At Hogwarts, Harry becomes friends with Ron Weasley and Hermione Granger, learns about the world of magic, and finds that he is a natural at the wizard sport Quidditch. Harry and his friends discover that the Sorcerer's Stone, which gives its owner immortality, is being guarded at Hogwarts. With help from Ron and Hermione, Harry learns that Professor Quirrell is trying to steal the Stone and that the evil wizard Voldemort is inhabiting Quirrell's body.

J. K. Rowling

Style, Technique, and Language

Style and Technique—Americanization: One of the greatest controversies surrounding *Harry Potter and the Sorcerer's Stone* concerns the Americanization of the text. The original British edition of the novel underwent many changes meant to make it more accessible to Americans, the most prominent of which was the title, which changed from *Harry Potter and the Philosopher's Stone* to *Harry Potter and the Sorcerer's Stone*. Rowling has said about the changes: "Arthur Levine, my American editor, and I decided that words should be altered only where we felt they would be incomprehensible, even in context, to an American reader. The title change was Arthur's idea initially, because he felt that the British title gave a misleading idea of the subject matter. We discussed several alternative titles and *Sorcerer's Stone* was my idea." Some critics object to the title change, which eliminates the reference to the ancient concept of the Philosopher's Stone, a stone thought to contain an elixir that would grant eternal life. Eliminating the reference, these critics suggest, points to an assumption that American intellect is feeble. These critics also object to the many smaller changes made throughout the text, arguing that American readers are perfectly capable of reading Tolkien, C. S. Lewis, and other British fantasy writers without translation, and are equally capable of reading Rowling's novel as she originally wrote it. Many of the changes in this first volume are only matters of spelling, but others are translations of words and phrases such as sherbet lemon (a type of hard candy), jumper (sweater), and comprehensive (high school). These small changes make *Harry Potter* more comprehensible to Americans, but they also leach some of the British sensibility from the text.

Language—Names: One of Rowling's great strengths as a fantasy writer is her skill at employing colorful names. Rowling has said, "I am a bit of a name freak. A lot of the names that I didn't invent come from maps. Snape is a place name in Britain. Dumbledore is an old English dialect word for bumblebee, because he is a musical person, and I imagine him humming to himself all the time. Hagrid is also an old English word. Hedwig was a medieval saint." Most of Rowling's characters have names that reflect their personalities. "Snape" is a near-homonym of "snake," and "Severus" is a Latin word meaning "severe." "Voldemort" comes from the French for "flight of death," while "Malfoy" comes from the French for "bad faith." Other names suggest the ruling moods of characters, such as "Peeves" and "Crabbe." Some names come from ancient mythology, such as "Argus Filch," whose first name is that of a legendary watchman.

Characters in *Harry Potter and the Sorcerer's Stone*

Bane: A black centaur who lives in the Forbidden Forest. He believes in the prophecy of the stars and thinks that centaurs should not interfere with foretold events.

Katie Bell: A Chaser for the Gryffindor Quidditch team.

Professor Binns: The only ghost teaching at Hogwarts, and the most boring of Harry's teachers. Binns teaches the History of Magic.

Bletchley: A Keeper for the Slytherin Quidditch team.

The Bloody Baron: A Slytherin ghost, and the only being who can control Peeves.

Lavender Brown: A friend of Parvati Patil.

Crabbe: One of Draco Malfoy's henchmen. Crabbe is constantly by Draco's side.

Doris Crockford: A fan of Harry's. Doris meets Harry in the Leaky Cauldron.

Dedalus Diggle: Another fan of Harry's.

Albus Dumbledore: Headmaster of Hogwarts. Dumbledore is a kind, understanding wizard who trusts Harry's judgment. He is the only wizard whom Voldemort fears.

Dudley Dursley: A spoiled cousin of Harry's. Dudley takes delight in being cruel to Harry. He throws frequent tantrums and breaks the toys his parents lavish upon him.

Petunia Dursley: Harry's aunt. Mrs. Dursley constantly fawns over her son, Dudley, and treats Harry like an unwanted servant. She resents the affection her parents showed her sister (Harry's mother), Lily Potter, who was a witch. Mrs. Dursley's abiding resentment toward Lily fuels her hostility toward her nephew and the wizarding world.

Vernon Dursley: Harry's uncle. Vernon, who works for a drill-making company, is self-centered, gruff, and impolite. He treats Harry rudely and cruelly, especially when Harry shows signs of having magical powers. Strongly prejudiced against the wizarding world, Vernon tries to block Harry's involvement in magic.

Fang: Hagrid's dog. Fang is a black boarhound.

The Fat Friar: A Hufflepuff ghost.

The Fat Lady: A figure in a portrait. She guards the entrance to the Gryffindor common room.

Mrs. Figg: An occasional babysitter for Harry. When Mrs. Figg breaks a leg tripping over one of her cats, an accident that leaves her incapacitated, Harry is allowed to accompany Dudley to the zoo.

Argus Filch: The caretaker at Hogwarts. A disagreeable sort, Argus is suspicious of Harry and his friends.

Seamus Finnigan: A first-year student in Gryffindor house. Seamus's father is a Muggle, and his mother is a witch.

Firenze: A white centaur who lives in the Forbidden Forest. Unlike the other centaurs, Firenze is willing to help Harry.

Nicolas Flamel: A partner in Albus Dumbledore's work on alchemy. Nicolas Flamel is 665 years old, thanks to the life-giving properties of the Sorcerer's Stone.

Marcus Flint: The captain of the Slytherin Quidditch team. Flint is a sixth-year student.

Professor Flitwick: The Charms teacher at Hogwarts.

Fluffy: A three-headed dog belonging to Hagrid. Fluffy guards the Sorcerer's Stone.

Cornelius Fudge: The Minister of Magic. Hagrid believes Cornelius to be a bungler.

Goyle: One of Draco Malfoy's henchmen.

Hermione Granger: A first-year student at Hogwarts and a close friend of Harry's. Though from a family of Muggles, Hermione excels at her academic studies. Her superior attitude sometimes alienates her peers, but she mellows somewhat as the year progresses.

Griphook: A goblin who escorts Harry and Hagrid through Gringotts, the wizards' bank.

Hagrid: The Keeper of Keys and Grounds at Hogwarts. Hagrid is a huge man with a special affection for Harry. Although simple-minded and disposed to reveal too much, Hagrid has the capacity to love others deeply.

Hedwig: Harry's snowy owl. Hedwig was a gift from Hagrid, who purchased her at Eeylops Owl Emporium in Diagon Alley.

Terence Higgs: The Seeker for the Slytherin Quidditch team.

Madam Hooch: The Quidditch coach at Hogwarts. Madam Hooch also gives flying lessons.

Angelina Johnson: A Chaser for the Gryffindor Quidditch team.

Lee Jordan: A student at Hogwarts and friend of the Weasleys. He does commentary for the Quidditch matches.

Neville Longbottom: A first-year student at Hogwarts. Neville is careless and easily intimidated, but gradually he becomes braver and eventually stands up to both Malfoy and his own friends. Neville was raised by his grandmother, who is a witch.

Madam Malkin: The proprietress of a robe shop in Diagon Alley.

Professor McGonagall: The "strict and clever" teacher of Transfiguration at Hogwarts. Professor McGonagall is the Head of Gryffindor house and has taken a special interest in Harry since his delivery to the Dursleys.

Nicholas de Mimsy-Porpington (Nearly Headless Nick): The Gryffindor ghost. He was killed by a botched decapitation that did not quite sever his neck.

Norbert: A Norwegian Ridgeback dragon and, briefly, Hagrid's pet.

Mrs. Norris: A cat belonging to Argus Filch.

Mr. Ollivander: Maker of magic wands and proprietor of a shop in Diagon Alley.

Pansy Parkinson: A Slytherin girl who takes Malfoy's side in arguments.

Parvati Patil: A first-year girl who is not afraid to stand up to Malfoy. Parvati has a twin sister.

Madam Pince: The librarian at Hogwarts.

Peeves: A mischievous poltergeist who inhabits Hogwarts.

Piers Polkiss: Dudley Dursley's best friend. Like Dudley, Piers delights in beating up Harry. Piers is at the zoo when Harry talks to the boa constrictor.

Madam Pomfrey: Hogwarts's school nurse. She heals injuries using magic.

Harry Potter: An eleven-year-old wizard. As an infant, Harry is left to live with his aunt and uncle after Voldemort murders his parents. Hagrid rescues him and takes him to Hogwarts, where Harry discovers that he is famous for surviving an attack by Voldemort, and that he possesses courage and skill at wizardry.

Lily and James Potter: The parents of Harry Potter. Both attended Hogwarts. Voldemort murdered them when Harry was an infant.

Adrian Pucey: a Chaser for the Slytherin Quidditch team.

Professor Quirrell: A stuttering teacher of Defense Against the Dark Arts at Hogwarts. Quirrell is an ineffective teacher, and some of the students think he is a fraud. Quirrell provides a host body for Voldemort and tries to steal the Sorcerer's Stone for the Dark wizard.

Ronan: A russet-haired centaur who lives in the Forbidden Forest. Ronan believes in the prophecy of the stars.

Scabbers: Ron Weasley's pet rat. Scabbers, a hand-me-down from Percy, is usually asleep.

Severus Snape: The Potions master at Hogwarts. Snape was James Potter's enemy when both men were schoolboys, but James saved Snape's life. As a result, Snape has mixed feelings for Harry Potter, exhibiting both distaste for and protectiveness toward him.

The Sorting Hat: A battered, talking wizard's hat that sorts new students into the four houses at Hogwarts.

Alicia Spinnet: A Chaser for the Gryffindor Quidditch team.

Professor Sprout: A teacher of Herbology at Hogwarts and the Head of Hufflepuff house.

Dean Thomas: A Gryffindor first year who sleeps in Harry and Ron's dormitory. Dean sometimes compares soccer, his favorite game, to Quidditch.

Trevor: Neville Longbottom's frog.

Voldemort: An evil wizard who, at the height of his powers, murdered many people and presided over a dark period in wizarding history. Voldemort disappeared after failing to kill Harry Potter ten years before the novel begins. He tries to regain his human form and obtain the Sorcerer's Stone.

Bill Weasley: One of Ron Weasley's older brothers. Formerly Head Boy at Hogwarts, Bill now studies dragons in Romania.

Charlie Weasley: One of Ron Weasley's older brothers. Formerly captain of Quidditch at Hogwarts, Charlie now works for Gringotts in Africa.

Fred and George Weasley: The Weasley twins. Fred and George are fond of playing practical jokes. They are Beaters for the Gryffindor Quidditch team.

Ginny Weasley: The youngest Weasley child. Ginny is not yet a student at Hogwarts. She comes to the station to see off her brothers and is star-struck by Harry Potter.

Mrs. Weasley: The matriarch of the Weasley family. Mrs. Weasley is kind to Harry, showing him how to reach the platform for the Hogwarts Express and knitting him a sweater for Christmas.

Ron Weasley: The youngest of the Weasley boys. Like Harry, Ron is a first-year at Hogwarts. The two boys meet on the Hogwarts Express and become best friends. Ron has a taste for adventure. He feels overshadowed by the accomplishments of his older brothers and worries about his family's poverty.

Percy Weasley: The third-eldest of the Weasley brothers. Percy is a student at Hogwarts and boasts about his position as prefect.

Oliver Wood: The captain and Keeper of the Gryffindor Quidditch team. Wood teaches Harry the game.

Reading *Harry Potter and the Sorcerer's Stone*

CHAPTER ONE
The Boy Who Lived

The Dursleys live on Privet Drive with their baby son, Dudley. One morning on his way to work, **Mr. Vernon Dursley** sees a cat reading a map, and several people wearing cloaks, sights that puzzle him. On his lunch break, he overhears cloaked strangers mention the Potters and "their son, **Harry**." Worried that these strangers might be referring to his wife **Petunia**'s sister and her family, Mr. Dursley starts to call home but changes his mind when he recalls how any mention of her sister upsets his wife. Leaving work, Mr. Dursley bumps into an old man in a cloak who calls him a Muggle and tells him he should celebrate because "You-Know-Who" has gone.

When Mr. Dursley returns home, he sees the cat he saw that morning now sitting on the garden wall. News reports tell of owls flying in the daytime and showers of shooting stars. Mr. Dursley asks his wife if she has heard from her sister, saying that the strange events of the day might be related to "her crowd." She gets angry, but confirms that her nephew is named Harry. Mr. Dursley reasons that the Potters will not intrude on his life, since they know what the Dursleys think of "their kind."

That night, around midnight, **Albus Dumbledore** appears on the street corner. He is a thin old man with a long silver beard. Pointing a device that looks like a cigarette lighter toward the streetlights, Dumbledore extinguishes them. He then addresses the cat, calling it **Professor McGonagall**. The cat turns into a woman and asks Dumbledore to confirm the rumors that You-Know-Who has gone. Dumbledore tells her it is silly to refer to him as You-Know-Who; they should call him by his real name, **Voldemort**. He confirms the rumor that Voldemort killed **Lily and James Potter** and then lost his powers by trying and failing to murder the Potters' infant son, Harry. Dumbledore intends to leave Harry with the Dursleys, because, he says, the boy will be so famous in "our world" that he could not have a normal childhood.

A flying motorcycle driven by a huge man named **Hagrid** descends from the sky. Hagrid carries a baby boy with a lightning-shaped scar on his forehead. Dumbledore places the baby on the Dursleys' doorstep with a letter. Hagrid cries as he says goodbye to the baby. With his "Put-Outer," Dumbledore relights the streetlights. He whispers "[g]ood luck" to the baby, who cannot know that at celebrations throughout the country, he is being hailed as "the boy who lived."

UNDERSTANDING AND INTERPRETING
Chapter One

Two Worlds: The two narratives of Chapter One—one that follows Mr. Dursley through his day, and one that relates Harry's arrival at the Dursleys' house—introduce us to the world of the novel, one in which a hidden magical realm exists alongside everyday England. Rowling juxtaposes ordinary details of suburban life with fantastical details of magical life. A traffic jam, the TV news, and a doughnut shop exist in the same world as a lamp-extinguishing "Put-Outer," a flying motorcycle, and a cat that transforms into a woman. Although the mundane and the magical worlds overlap, most ordinary humans seem unaware of the presence of the magical realm. Others, such as the Dursleys, are grudgingly aware of its existence but do their best to ignore any evidence of it. When Mr. Dursley sees a cat reading a map and several people wearing cloaks, for example, he tries to explain away what he has seen, convincing himself that his eyes are playing tricks on him and that cloaks must be a new fashion.

The Instant Hero: The story of infant Harry's defeat of the sinister Voldemort, combined with Dumbledore's conviction that Harry's fame will prohibit a normal childhood, immediately identify Harry as a hero in a long battle of good over evil. Rowling's novel follows in a long literary tradition of stories in which children are the heroes of great adventures, stories such as *Treasure Island* and *The Chronicles of Narnia*. Rowling's novel, unlike many other novels in the genre, identifies Harry as a hero right away. Although Harry's fame goes unnoticed for most of his childhood, once it becomes known, he must struggle not only to earn continued acclaim but to overcome the annoyances that accompany notoriety.

CHAPTER TWO
The Vanishing Glass

The narrative jumps to ten years after the deposit of the infant Harry on the Dursleys' steps. Mr. and Mrs. Dursley ignore Harry and force him to live in the cupboard under the stairs while they spoil their son, **Dudley**, with lavish gifts and overindulgence. Harry must wear Dudley's enormous hand-me-down clothes and a pair of glasses mended with Scotch tape. One morning, his aunt wakes him from a dream about a flying motorcycle and makes him help prepare breakfast for Dudley's birthday. Dudley arrives in the kitchen, counts his presents, and complains that there are only thirty-seven, one less than the previous year. Mrs. Dursley promises to buy him two more.

Mrs. Dursley finds out that **Mrs. Figg**, with whom Harry was to spend the day, has broken her leg. In consequence, the Dursleys must take Harry along on Dudley's birthday excursion to the zoo. Mr. Dursley warns Harry not to pull any "funny business." Harry thinks of past occasions when odd things happened to him. Doing his best to steer clear of Dudley and Dudley's friend **Piers Polkiss**, both of whom enjoy hitting him, Harry has a wonderful day.

After lunch, the group visits the reptile house. When Dudley tells his father to make a giant boa constrictor move, Mr. Dursley taps on the glass, but nothing happens. Then Harry stands in front of the snake's cage alone, and the snake lifts its head and winks, which only Harry notices. Harry finds he can communicate with the snake by talking to it and watching it gesture back. When Harry asks the snake where it comes from, it points with its tail to a sign that reads, "Boa Constrictor, Brazil."

Piers calls to the others to come and see the snake's amazing behavior. Dudley shoves Harry out of the way, and Harry falls to the floor. When he looks up, the glass of the snake's tank is gone, and the snake is slithering away. Harry thinks he hears the snake announce plans to head to Brazil. When they return home, Mr. Dursley is furious to hear from Piers that Harry was talking to the snake. He sends Harry to his cupboard without dinner. In the darkness, Harry tries to remember the car crash that, according to his aunt and uncle, killed his parents. All he can remember is a flash of green light and an injury to his forehead. He thinks of times when oddly dressed strangers seemed to know him.

UNDERSTANDING AND INTERPRETING
Chapter Two

Fitting In and Breaking Out: Rowling endears Harry to readers by giving him familiar problems. Harry, forced to live under the stairs in the household of a family that hates him, suffers from an exaggeratedly difficult situation, but his feelings are universal. Harry's adopted parents ignore him, and his pseudo-sibling bullies him. He wonders about his "real" parents, feels like a freak in his own family, and longs for someone to rescue him. He is, in short, like virtually every other adolescent in the world.

It's the Little Things: In the first two chapters of *Harry Potter and the Sorcerer's Stone*, Rowling includes details that become pertinent in later novels in the series. Harry's conversation with the boa constrictor becomes important in the second novel, for example. In Chapter One, Hagrid rode a motorcycle borrowed from Sirius Black, who reappears in the third novel. The inclusion of details that become important only much later indicate the degree to which Rowling imagined the series as a whole. Perhaps, too, the inclusion of seemingly trivial facts suggests that in life as well as in fiction, it is wise to pay attention to details, for they might become significant in the future.

CHAPTER THREE
The Letters from No One

Harry is incarcerated in his cupboard for the longest time yet as punishment for the episode at the zoo. When he emerges, the summer holidays have begun, and Harry spends his time trying to avoid Dudley and his gang of thugs. Harry looks forward to September, when he will attend the local public school and Dudley will go to a private school, Smeltings. Mrs. Dursley takes Dudley to buy his Smeltings uniform. The next day, she dyes some of Dudley's old clothes gray to serve as Harry's uniform.

Harry gets a letter in the mail one day, the first he has ever received. It is addressed to "Mr. H. Potter, The Cupboard under the Stairs." Before Harry can read the letter, Mr.Dursley snatches it from him. He and his wife read it, look horrified, and send the boys out of the room. Harry and Dudley eavesdrop on the grownups' mysterious conversation, which ends with Mr. Dursley proclaiming he will not have "one in the house." Mr. Dursley tells Harry the letter was addressed incorrectly and he has burned it. He invites Harry to move from the cupboard into Dudley's second bedroom, where Dudley has been storing his toys.

The next day another letter arrives, this one directed to "Mr. H. Potter, The Smallest Bedroom." Mr. Dursley confiscates it and sends the boys away. The next morning, Harry rises at six to sneak out and meet the postman at the corner, but Mr. Dursley has slept by the front door and catches Harry. Three letters arrive, but Mr. Dursley destroys them all and nails the mail slot shut. The next day, twelve letters arrive, mostly through the cracks around the door. Mr. Dursley boards up these cracks. The next day, twenty-four letters arrive, one inside each of the eggs delivered by the milkman. Though the next day is Sunday, when no mail is delivered, thirty or forty letters come flying out of the fireplace.

Mr. Dursley announces that the family is going away. They drive all day and spend the night at a dreary hotel. The next morning, the hotel owner brings a letter addressed to Harry to the table and reports that he has a hundred more at the front desk. For the rest of the day, Mr. Dursley drives the family to various isolated locations. He finally settles on the coast, where he borrows a rowboat to take the family to a desolate shack on an offshore rock. They bed down for the night as a storm begins to brew.

Harry can't sleep. He watches the hands on Dudley's watch creep toward midnight, when it will be Harry's eleventh birthday. As Harry lies awake, he hears strange noises outside. At the stroke of midnight, there is a loud knock at the door.

UNDERSTANDING AND INTERPRETING
Chapter Three

Dursley Loses His Grip: Chapter Three shows Mr. Dursley actively trying to deny and subvert Harry's identity. The attempt to keep Harry from discovering his true nature drives Mr. Dursley to the brink of insanity and causes him to increasingly isolate his family. Most adolescents occasionally feel that their parents are denying them their identity or attempting to control it, so Mr. Dursley's irrational behavior elicits readers' sympathy for Harry.

Ignoring Dudley: The degree to which Mr. Dursley feels threatened by Harry's identity is made clear by his new willingness to cause Dudley unhappiness. From the moment the first letter arrives, Dudley ceases to be the focus of attention in the house, a previously unthinkable shift. Mr. Dursley moves Harry into Dudley's second bedroom, an action calculated either to appease or to fool the letter-writer, with no concern for Dudley's preference. During the long journey, Mr. Dursley ignores Dudley's complaints, which he has never done before. Dudley assumes his father has gone mad, not just because of his maniacal insistence on isolation, but because of his sudden, inexplicable refusal to cater to Dudley's every whim.

CHAPTER FOUR
The Keeper of the Keys

Mr. Dursley rushes into the room with a rifle in time to see the door knocked off its hinges by "a giant of a man" who comes into the room, asks for a cup of tea, and warmly addresses Harry. Mr. Dursley interrupts, telling the giant to leave, but the giant tells him to shut up and bends Vernon's gun into a knot. The giant gives Harry a birthday cake and introduces himself as "Rubeus Hagrid, Keeper of Keys and Grounds at Hogwarts."

Hagrid makes a fire in the fireplace and takes from his coat his own provisions for making tea. He cooks sausages over the fire and hands them to Harry, who eats hungrily. Hagrid soon realizes, to his shock, that Harry has never heard of Hogwarts and knows nothing about the fame of his parents or himself. Mr. Dursley tries to stop Hagrid from saying more, but Hagrid ignores him and announces that Harry is a wizard.

Hagrid gives Harry a letter from Minerva McGonagall, accepting Harry into Hogwarts School of Witchcraft and Wizardry. After scrawling a note to the Hogwarts Headmaster, Albus Dumbledore, Hagrid pulls an owl from a coat pocket and sends it flying off with the message. Mr. Dursley insists Harry will not go to Hogwarts, but Hagrid scoffs at the idea that a Muggle could stop him, explaining that "Muggle" is a term for non-magical people. Mr. Dursley exclaims he and Mrs. Dursley have determined to eradicate wizardry from Harry, and Mrs. Dursley complains bitterly that her sister, Lily, got all the attention in the family because she was a witch.

Hagrid tells Harry the truth about his parents' deaths. A wizard named Voldemort "went bad" and became very powerful, killing anyone who opposed him. Harry's parents, who as students had been Head Boy and Girl at Hogwarts, opposed Voldemort. On Halloween, when Harry was one year old, Voldemort killed the Potters, tried and failed to kill Harry, and then mysteriously disappeared. Harry was the first person to survive an attack by Voldemort.

Harry says that there must be a mistake—he is not a wizard. Hagrid asks Harry if he has ever made things happen in fear or anger, and Harry realizes he has. For example, he set the snake loose at the zoo when he got angry with Dudley. When Mr. Dursley again insists that he will not pay for Harry to go to Hogwarts and calls Dumbledore a "crackpot old fool," Hagrid becomes furious. He points his umbrella at Dudley, and the boy sprouts a pig's tail. The Dursleys flee the room.

Hagrid confesses to Harry that he was expelled from Hogwarts in his third year and is not supposed to perform magic. When Harry asks Hagrid why he was expelled, Hagrid changes the subject, telling Harry there is much to do the next day.

UNDERSTANDING AND INTERPRETING
Chapter Four

Petunia Tells Her Tale: In this chapter, Mrs. Dursley speaks at length, and for the first time, we realize that something specific caused her nastiness, which enables us to sympathize with her at least a little bit. Mrs. Dursley's speech marks her most human moment, for in it she expresses envy of a sibling, an almost universal feeling. It still irks Mrs. Dursley that her parents favored the magical Lily, even though Lily was a "freak," and she, Petunia, was normal. Instead of learning from her own childhood to treat both of the children she raises equally, Mrs. Dursley repeats the mistakes made by her parents. She mistreats Harry terribly and showers her Muggle son with affection. Though Mrs. Dursley's speech wins her a modicum of sympathy, it also reveals how weak she is in comparison to Harry. Mrs. Dursley responds to a favored sibling with hatred, holding a grudge against her for decades. Harry responds to a favored sibling with annoyance but never with hatred. Harry dislikes Dudley and does his best to avoid him, but he does not feel for him the festering resentment that Mrs. Dursley feels for Lily.

In the Midst of the Battle: Many novels begin *in medias res*, a Latin phrase meaning "in the middle of things," as a way of catching readers' interest immediately. Though this novel begins when Harry is a baby, it also begins in the middle of a battle larger than Harry. Harry does not understand this battle, and neither do we, because Rowling gives us only as much information as Harry has. She puts us in his shoes. By making us identify with Harry, and giving us only as much information as Harry has, Rowling makes understanding that battle as difficult for us as it is for Harry. We finally find out the true history of Harry and his parents in this chapter, when Hagrid explains everything to Harry.

Harry and Hagrid: From the beginning of the novel, Harry and Hagrid enjoy a special bond. Hagrid acts as a surrogate parent to Harry, leaving him on the Dursleys' doorstep and weeping over him as a father would. Ten years later, Hagrid provides the link between the Muggle world and the wizarding world. He tells Harry the story of his parents, softening its violence with kindness and visible love for Lily and James Potter. Hagrid feeds Harry sausages and birthday cake and ignores the Dursleys. This nurturing gesture marks the first time that someone important and powerful has shown the Dursleys that Harry is an interesting person more worthy of respect than they are. From Hagrid, Harry gets everything the Dursleys deny him: attention, respect, and love.

Universal Wish Fulfilled: Harry's rescue at the hands of Hagrid is both familiar and deeply foreign. It is familiar because most people who feel alienated or freakish when young eventually discover that there are others like them and they have never been truly alone. When Harry receives the letters and the surprise visit from Hagrid, he realizes for the first time that the Dursleys do not define normality. Harry's rescue is foreign, however, because it so literally embodies a universal childhood wish. Most children at some point are convinced that they belong to some other family—not the undesirable one in which they find themselves—and are ultimately disappointed to learn that their family is truly theirs. Harry, on the other hand, really *does* belong to another family. Many children also long for a fearsome protector who will punish those who mistreat them. Few children ever attain such a formidable ally, but Harry gets the magnificent Hagrid.

CHAPTER FIVE
Diagon Alley

Harry wakes the next morning convinced that the events of the night before were a dream. He opens his eyes and sees Hagrid sleeping on the couch and an owl waiting at the window, holding the *Daily Prophet* newspaper. Hagrid wakes and instructs Harry to take five bronze coins from Hagrid's coat and pay the owl. Harry tells Hagrid that he has no money to pay for Hogwarts. Hagrid comforts Harry, telling him his inheritance is in a goblin-run bank, Gringotts. Harry and Hagrid leave the shack on the boat Mr. Dursley rented the night before. Hagrid suggests using magic to speed up the trip, even though he is not supposed to, and Harry agrees not to tell. Hagrid explains there is a Ministry of Magic that works to keep the wizarding world hidden from Muggles.

ART FOR ADULTS

In Britain, the publisher of Rowling's books noted that many adults were reading the Harry Potter series. He thought that perhaps even more adults were interested in the series, but stayed away from it out of embarrassment at the prospect of being seen reading children's books. In order to attract a larger group of adult readers, the publisher put out a new edition of the Harry Potter series, this one featuring covers with adult artwork. Unlike the colorful, cartoonish covers originally used in the Harry Potter series, these alternate covers use black-and-white photographs and stark artwork.

On the train to London, Harry looks at the list of things he will need for his first year at Hogwarts—a magic wand, a cauldron, books about magic, robes, and so on. In London, Hagrid takes Harry to a small, dirty pub called the Leaky Cauldron. Harry suspects that only he and Hagrid can see the pub, since Muggle passersby do not notice it. Inside, the bartender and the patrons realize who Harry is and gather around to shake his hand. Harry meets **Professor Quirrell**, a stuttering man who teaches Defense Against the Dark Arts at Hogwarts.

Hagrid takes Harry to a courtyard behind the pub, where he taps a wall with his umbrella. An opening appears, leading into Diagon Alley, a street filled with shops for wizards and witches. Harry and Hagrid proceed to Gringotts, where a goblin named **Griphook** takes them on a rapid cart ride through a maze of underground passages. They arrive at Harry's vault, where Harry discovers heaps of gold Galleons, silver Sickles, and bronze Knuts—all his. He takes a bag of coins and they go to Vault 713, where Hagrid, on an errand for Albus Dumbledore, removes a small package.

Hagrid leaves Harry to be fitted for robes by **Madam Malkin**. In her shop, Harry meets a snobby boy also headed for his first year at Hogwarts. The boy talks about racing brooms, a game called Quidditch, and Slytherin, the house at Hogwarts to which everyone in his family has belonged. The boy calls Hagrid a savage and says that Hogwarts should only accept students from old wizarding families who have been brought up in the wizarding traditions. Hagrid meets Harry outside and, in answer to his questions, explains that Quidditch is played on flying brooms, and Hogwarts is divided into four houses. Slytherin is the house that produces all of the witches and wizards that ever "went bad," including Voldemort, who was once a student at Hogwarts.

Hagrid buys Harry an owl. At **Mr. Ollivander's** shop, Harry tries out scores of wands until he finds the one that shoots sparks when he waves it. Mr. Ollivander explains that wands choose their wizards, and oddly, the wand that chose Harry is the brother of the wand that gave Harry his scar. Hagrid takes Harry back to the train station so he can return to the Dursleys. He gives Harry a ticket for a train that will take him to Hogwarts on September 1.

UNDERSTANDING AND INTERPRETING
Chapter Five

Worlds Collide: By the end of Chapter Five, Rowling has fully established the existence of two parallel, sometimes overlapping worlds: the Muggle world Harry has known for most of his life, and the magical world of wizards. Although members of the two worlds sometimes interact, the magical world is strange to novices such as Harry, just as the Muggle world is strange to creatures from the magical world such as Hagrid. Harry spends most of Chapter Five goggling at the new sights he sees in Diagon Alley, and Hagrid spends a great deal of time marveling at the strangeness of everyday England. Just as Harry wonders at magic wands, Quidditch, and flying brooms, Hagrid wonders at parking meters, the Underground, and the ability of Muggles to survive without magic.

Delighting in the Details: Rowling's magical world delights not because of its extreme difference from the everyday world—in its morality, social structure, and economic system, it is just like the everyday world—but as a result of its details. Boys peer in a window at the latest sporting goods, students try on new clothes as they prepare to go back to school, and schoolboys preen in front of one another. These actions please us because they are entirely familiar ones made exotic with a little twist of the magical: the boys are peering at brooms, not footballs; trying on robes, not shirts; and touting their skill at Quidditch, not soccer.

Racism and Class Snobbery: Harry's brief exchange with the boy in the robe shop shows that prejudice familiar from the everyday world also exists in the wizarding world. The boy expresses racist sentiments, saying that privilege and acceptance in the magical world should be based on bloodline. His attitudes also parody the stereotyped snobbery of upper-class England. The Hogwarts-bound boy shuddering at the thought of Muggle classmates sounds just like an Oxford-bound boy shuddering at the thought of riff-raff sneaking into his peer group. The conceitedness of the boy reminds Harry of Dudley, but the boy's racism and class snobbery is much more sinister than Dudley's whining narcissism.

CHAPTER SIX
The Journey from Platform Nine and Three-Quarters

Harry spends an awkward month with the Dursleys, who ignore him completely. The day before school is to begin, Harry asks Mr. Dursley for a ride to King's Cross Station. Mr. Dursley consents, since he is already taking Dudley to London to have his pig's tail removed. The next day, in London, Mr. Dursley takes Harry's trunk into the station for him and points out that there are no platforms between nine and ten, even though Harry's ticket says his train will depart from platform nine and three-quarters. The Dursleys drive away laughing, leaving Harry alone with his owl, whom he has named **Hedwig**.

Harry sees a family with an owl and follows them. He watches as the children in the family disappear, one after another, between platforms nine and ten. The mother, **Mrs. Weasley**, sees Harry, realizes he must be a first-year student at Hogwarts, and kindly instructs him to walk straight toward the barrier between the platforms. He does this and finds himself on platform nine and three-quarters, next to the Hogwarts Express. Twin brothers **Fred** and **George Weasley** help Harry carry his trunk onto the train. They notice his scar and tell the rest of their family that he is Harry Potter.

The youngest boy in the family, **Ron**, comes and sits in Harry's compartment. Fred and George come in for a moment and introduce themselves as Ron's brothers. When they leave, Ron asks about Harry's scar and stares at Harry in fascination. Harry, self-conscious about his fame, asks Ron about his family. Ron talks about his five older brothers and the pressure he feels to succeed at Hogwarts. He introduces his rat, **Scabbers**, nearly admitting that he has a rat because his parents could not afford an owl. Harry expresses his own insecurities about Hogwarts, saying he knows nothing about the wizarding world or magic.

When a woman appears in the corridor with a cartful of treats, Harry buys a heap of candy and enjoys sharing it with Ron. In his Chocolate Frog wrapper, Harry finds a trading card with a picture of Albus Dumbledore, Hogwarts' Headmaster. The card calls Dumbledore "the greatest wizard of modern times" and mentions his work on alchemy with Nicolas Flamel. A boy enters their compartment looking for his lost toad. He returns later with a girl in time to witness Ron's failed attempt to cast a spell on Scabbers. The girl, **Hermione Granger**, says she has already memorized all of the course books. She hopes to be put in Gryffindor house but says Ravenclaw "wouldn't be too bad."

Hermione leaves, and Ron tells Harry about an attempted robbery at Gringotts. He also tries to explain Quidditch. Three boys enter the compartment— **Draco Malfoy**, the snob Harry met at the robe shop, and his friends **Crabbe** and **Goyle**. Malfoy, who has just learned who Harry is, tells Harry he should not make friends with "the wrong sort." Insulted on Ron's behalf, Harry refuses to shake Malfoy's hand. When Malfoy insults both the Weasleys and Hagrid, Harry and Ron prepare to fight him and his cronies. Goyle tries to take some of Harry's Chocolate Frogs, and Scabbers bites him. Malfoy, Crabbe, and Goyle leave.

Hermione returns and tells the boys to put on their robes; the journey is almost over. They arrive at a dark station, and Hagrid meets the first-year students and puts them into boats that take them across a lake to the castle of Hogwarts. Hagrid finds the missing toad, which belongs to **Neville Longbottom**, and brings the students to the front door.

UNDERSTANDING AND INTERPRETING
Chapter Six

Back to School: For their own reasons, Ron and Harry both experience anxiety about starting at a new school. Ron, like many young siblings in large families, feels pressure to live up to the standards of success established by his older brothers. He is familiar with the way Hogwarts operates, but that familiarity only heightens his unease. He knows exactly what is expected of him and worries that he will fail. Harry feels anxious for different reasons. He worries that he is the only student on the train who is wholly ignorant of the world of magic. Unlike Ron, Harry has no idea what is expected of him. He feels added pressure because of his fame. How will it look, he worries, when the famous Harry Potter does not have even a rudimentary knowledge of the magical world? Ron's and Harry's anxiety, although centered around magic, is familiar to anyone who has ever experienced the stress of going to a new school.

The Pleasures of Friendship: Before now, Harry has never had a friend. On the train, he experiences for the first time some of the joys that come with friendship. Realizing that the Weasleys are not well-off and cannot afford expensive treats, Harry eagerly shares his food with Ron. Later, when confronted with Malfoy and his cohorts, Harry discovers the pleasures of fighting with a friend by your side. Dudley familiarized Harry with the tactics of bullies, but never before has Harry had the experience of teaming up with a friend to oppose bullies.

CHAPTER SEVEN
The Sorting Hat

McGonagall tells the first-years they must be sorted into the four Hogwarts houses. Each student's house will be like a family. Triumphs earn points for one's house, while transgressions lose points. At the end of the year, the house with the most points wins the house cup. Harry worries that being sorted into houses will involve taking a test. It does not comfort him that the other students look as frightened as he feels. A group of ghosts passes through the room on the way to the Great Hall, chatting among themselves and startling the students.

Professor McGonagall ushers the students into the Great Hall, where candles hang in the air and the ceiling is enchanted to look like the sky outside. She places the **Sorting Hat**, an old wizard's hat, on a stool. The hat sings a song praising the virtues of the four houses. Harry feels some relief when he realizes that the new students only have to try on the hat.

Students place the hat on their heads, one at a time, and the hat shouts out a house for each student. Hermione is assigned to Gryffindor and takes her seat at the Gryffindor table. Harry worries that he will not be chosen for any house. When his name is called, the students whisper among themselves as they realize that he is the famous Harry Potter. Harry puts on the hat and hears its thoughts. Silently, Harry wishes not to be assigned to Slytherin. The hat hears his thoughts and tells him that Slytherin would help him become great, but if he is sure, Gryffindor it will be. The hat calls out "GRYFFINDOR!" Ron, too, is assigned to Gryffindor.

The sorting is followed by an extravagant feast, which appears magically on the table. Harry meets the Gryffindor ghost, Sir Nicholas de Mimsy-Porpington, also known as **Nearly Headless Nick** because he was killed in a botched decapitation. Nick hopes that this year, Gryffindor will win the house cup, which Slytherin has won six years in a row. Harry sees a teacher with a hooked nose talking to Professor Quirrell, who is wearing a turban. The hook-nosed teacher looks into Harry's eyes, and Harry's scar suddenly begins to hurt. **Percy Weasley** remarks that the teacher is **Professor Snape**, who teaches Potions.

> "What J.K. Rowling has done, with considerable charm and inventive brio, is to take the traditional rituals of English public schools and show them in a light in which they seem as curious to outsiders as the rites of passage of tribal Africa. She makes it easy to overlook the fact that the most visible character going through Harry Potter's training even now is Harry Windsor."
>
> **PICO IYER**, "THE PLAYING FIELDS OF HOGWARTS"

Dumbledore tells the students that both the forest outside the castle and a corridor on the third floor are off limits. Everyone sings the school song, each to his own favorite tune. Percy leads the new Gryffindors toward their dormitories. They arrive at a portrait of **the Fat Lady**, who asks for the password, which Percy gives: "Caput Draconis." The portrait swings out, allowing the students into the Gryffindor common room. From there, the boys and girls climb to their respective dormitories. Harry has a nightmare about Malfoy and Snape trying to coax him into Slytherin, which he forgets by morning.

THE HOUSE SYSTEM

The house system at British boarding schools has its roots in Celtic monasteries. In the seventh and eighth centuries, monks educated the sons of wealthy noblemen. Each monk taught his students in his own hut or house. When schooling became more formalized, many private schools maintained the practice of assigning their students to houses.

UNDERSTANDING AND INTERPRETING
Chapter Seven

The Boarding School Novel: Rowling models Hogwarts on typical British boarding schools. Novels set in boarding schools have been popular in Britain since the 1857 publication of *Tom Brown's School Days*, so British readers can immediately locate Harry in a literary tradition and appreciate the humor of a magic school that is, in most ways, exactly like an ordinary boarding school. American readers will probably be less familiar than British readers with the boarding school novel and the traditions of British boarding schools. Many boarding schools in Britain accept students as young as nine or ten years old, which means that the boarding school novel often chronicles the life of a very young protagonist. This contrasts with America prep school novels such as *The Catcher in the Rye* and *A Separate Peace*, which focus on the transition from adolescence to adulthood. Many British schools are divided into houses, as Hogwarts is. Students are assigned to these houses, which compete in intra-school sports.

Sorting Harry: Harry's encounter with the Sorting Hat, while brief, is revelatory. Harry dreads putting on the hat because he fears it will assign him to Slytherin, which he associates with unlikable students. He assumes that the hat alone decides the students' fate and does not care what the students desire. But when Harry puts on the hat, he finds that the process of choosing a house—and thereby choosing whether to belong to a good or to an evil place—involves a negotiation. The hat tempts Harry with Slytherin, telling him that Slytherin will make him powerful, but it is willing to accept Harry's desire to live in Gryffindor. This interaction is a miniature display of the role of fate in Harry's life. The hat, which stands for fate, decides much of Harry's life for him. Harry is a wizard, and he must attend Hogwarts and live in a house there. These things have been decided for him. However, Harry has control over what he does with his given powers. The hat says that Harry *could* be great in Slytherin rather than saying he *will* be great, as if to emphasize Harry's freedom to do with his potential what he wishes. In letting Harry choose between the dark Slytherin and the noble Gryffindor, the hat allows Harry to make a larger symbolic choice between goodness and wickedness.

CHAPTER EIGHT
The Potions Master

Chapter Eight introduces us to Harry's everyday life at Hogwarts. Harry is surprised by how much the students have to learn. Hermione is the most proficient first-year. Professor Quirrell seems an incompetent teacher and tells his students an unlikely story about why he constantly wears a turban.

One day at breakfast, Harry receives an invitation to tea from Hagrid. That day, the Gryffindors have double Potions with Professor Snape. Snape picks on Harry, calling him a "celebrity" during roll call. He begins class by asking Harry a series of questions. Hermione raises her hand eagerly, but Harry does not know any of the answers. When Harry finally suggests that Snape ask Hermione, Snape takes a point from Gryffindor for his impertinence.

The students work in pairs on a potion for curing boils. Neville's potion goes horribly wrong, melting **Seamus Finnigan's** cauldron and covering Neville with boils. Snape blames Harry for not advising Neville on the procedure and takes another point from Gryffindor. After class, Harry and Ron go to Hagrid's tiny cabin on the grounds for tea. They meet Hagrid's huge dog, **Fang**. When Harry says that Snape seems to hate him, Hagrid changes the subject. Harry reads a newspaper clipping and discovers that the break-in at Gringotts happened on the same day that he and Hagrid visited the bank. The robbery was unsuccessful because the burgled vault had been emptied earlier that day. When Harry points this out, Hagrid says nothing. Harry leaves, wondering what secrets about Snape and Gringotts Hagrid is withholding.

UNDERSTANDING AND INTERPRETING
Chapter Eight

Background and Foreground: Each of the Harry Potter novels consists of two concurrent stories: the story of Harry's discovery of the wizarding world and his progress at Hogwarts, and the story of his growing conflict with Voldemort. Although Harry's scholastic progress could be considered mere background for his clash with Voldemort, Rowling makes both stories equally exciting. By Chapter Eight, the novel is almost half over, but Rowling has only hinted at the grand battle between good and evil that is to come, choosing to focus first on the routine of Harry's life at Hogwarts.

An Ordinary Boy: Rowling continues to show that, while Harry has great potential, he is ordinary in many ways. Harry's fame does not automatically grant him stupendous wizarding skills. Like his peers, Harry is just beginning at Hogwarts and must learn how to use magic. Like most students, Harry has trouble in his classes, does not like all of his teachers, and gets annoyed by students who seem to know how to do everything perfectly. The fact that Harry is flawed makes it easier for us to relate to him.

CHAPTER NINE
The Midnight Duel

The Gryffindors and the Slytherins have their first flying lesson together. **Madam Hooch**, the teacher, warns the students to fly only a few feet above the ground, but Neville accidentally rises far into the sky. He falls to the ground, breaking his wrist. Madam Hooch tells the students not to fly while she takes Neville to the hospital wing. In the grass, Malfoy finds Neville's Remembrall, a small sphere that glows red when the owner has forgotten something. When Harry tries to reclaim the Remembrall for Neville, Malfoy takes off on his broom. In violation of the rules, Harry flies after him. Harry quickly discovers that although he has never had flying lessons before, he instinctively knows how to fly. Below, the students gasp in amazement at Harry's skill. Malfoy tosses the Remembrall high into the air. Harry makes his broom dive and catches the sphere just before it hits the ground. Professor McGonagall spots him and marches him away. Harry feels certain he is going to be expelled and is surprised when McGonagall introduces him to **Oliver Wood**, the captain of the Gryffindor Quidditch team. Instead of being punished, Harry is made Seeker of the team because of his flying skills.

At dinner, Malfoy challenges Harry to a wizard's duel at midnight in the trophy room. Hermione overhears the challenge and tells Harry he should not break rules by going out at night, because if he gets caught, he will lose Gryffindor points. Harry, eager to defeat Malfoy, ignores her. Hermione follows Harry and Ron out of the portrait hole that night, still trying to discourage them. When she discovers that the Fat Lady is missing, and she cannot reenter the common room, Hermione follows the boys. The group comes across Neville, whose wrist is healed. Neville could not remember the password to get into Gryffindor tower.

The four students arrive in the trophy room, but Malfoy does not show up. Instead, the group narrowly escapes being discovered by the caretaker, **Filch**. As they run away from Filch, they encounter the Hogwarts poltergeist, **Peeves**, who calls out loudly that there are students out of bed. Hermione uses Harry's wand to unlock a door, and the students find themselves in the forbidden third-floor corridor, facing a giant three-headed dog. They run back to Gryffindor tower. Hermione suspects that the dog was standing on a trap door and is guarding something. Harry guesses that the dog is guarding the package Hagrid removed from Gringotts.

UNDERSTANDING AND INTERPRETING
Chapter Nine

The Benefit of Rule-Breaking: Harry makes progress in these chapters by breaking school rules, which reveals the novel's ambivalent position on obedience. First, Harry flouts Madam Hooch's instructions by flying. Later, he breaks rules by going out at night and venturing down the third-floor corridor. The latter transgression goes unpunished, and the former is rewarded. In front of the other students, Professor McGonagall scolds Harry for breaking school rules, but privately, she admires Harry, which becomes clear when she marches him straight to the Quidditch captain and praises his amazing flying skills. The idea that a little rule-breaking may be acceptable—even desirable—complicates the morality of the novel, as it complicates Harry. Harry is essentially good, but he is curious and has a streak of rebelliousness.

Hermione Steps Out: Until now, we have known Hermione primarily as an overly eager student willing to castigate Harry and Ron for breaking the rules. The final section of Chapter Eight, however, reveals new facets of her character. For the first time, Hermione joins Harry and Ron in an adventure. She shows the practical applications of her academic prowess by using magic to open a locked door. Hermione also impresses with her cool head. While Harry, Ron, and Neville cower in front of the three-headed dog, Hermione remains calm enough to observe the room. She notices the trap door and concludes that the dog is guarding something.

CHAPTER TEN
Halloween

Harry and Ron are eager for more adventures, but Hermione refuses to speak to them. A week later, Professor McGonagall sends Harry a Nimbus Two Thousand broom for use in Quidditch. When Malfoy confronts Harry, saying first-years are not allowed brooms, **Professor Flitwick** arrives and mentions the "special circumstances" permitting Harry's broom. Malfoy is horrified.

Oliver Wood teaches Harry the basics of Quidditch. Three Chasers try to put a ball called a Quaffle through one of three hoops. Each basket is worth ten points. A Keeper guards the hoops against the opposing Chasers. Two Bludgers, balls that fly on their own, zoom around, trying to knock players off their brooms. Two Beaters use bats to hit the Bludgers toward the other team. A Seeker tries to catch the tiny, fast-moving Golden Snitch. Catching the Snitch ends the game and earns the winning team 150 points.

In Charms class on Halloween, Hermione is the only one who can make a feather fly. She corrects Ron's technique, which annoys Ron. Later, he tells Harry that Hermione is "a nightmare," and no one likes her. Hermione over-hears and begins to cry. She is missing all afternoon, and Ron hears that she is in the girls' bathroom, crying.

Quirrell dashes into the Halloween feast, dramatically announcing there is a troll in the dungeons. Chaos erupts. Dumbledore tells the prefects to take the stu-dents to their dormitories. Harry and Ron realize that Hermione does not know about the troll, and they go to warn her. They see Snape heading for the third floor just before they spot the twelve-foot troll down the hall. When it enters a room, they close and lock the door behind it. Only when they hear a scream do they realize they have locked the troll in the girls' bathroom with Hermione.

They enter the bathroom and begin throwing things at the troll to confuse it. Harry jumps on the troll's back, and Ron casts a spell that makes the troll's club fly into the air and hit the troll on the head. The troll collapses on the floor. McGonagall, Snape, and Quirrell arrive. McGonagall is furious at the boys, but Hermione says she had gone to face the troll on her own, and Harry and Ron saved her. McGonagall takes five points from Gryffindor for Hermione's misbe-havior but awards five points each to Harry and Ron. Harry, Ron, and Hermione thank each other briefly. From then on, they are steadfast friends.

UNDERSTANDING AND INTERPRETING
Chapter Ten

The Greater Good: With Hermione's lie, Rowling reinforces the idea that some-times, rules must be broken. Because Hermione is naturally inclined toward obedience to authority, it matters more when she breaks rules than when Harry or Ron break them. Hermione, effectively deciding that friendship is more important than obedience, deceives McGonagall and takes responsibility for the dangerous confrontation with the troll. As the novel continues, Harry, Ron, and Hermione will have to decide when to break rules and when to follow them.

Vulnerable Wizards: The appearance of the troll sheds light on the workings of Hogwarts. The troll causes alarm at Hogwarts even though the school itself houses many bizarre, frightening creatures. Professor Quirrell, flustered at the best of times, is deeply shaken by the presence of the monster. The students are rushed off to the safety of their dormitories. It becomes clear that, despite the Hogwarts professors' mastery of magic, they are not invincible. Harry, who has been awed by the majesty of Hogwarts, now sees evidence that Hogwarts has spots of vulnerability and may need help.

High Stakes: For the second chapter in a row, Harry and his friends have an adventure outside the realm of normal school life. This time, though, they are not mere observers as they were in the third-floor corridor. Instead, Harry and Ron act. In the corridor, they faced Filch. In the bathroom, they face a troll who could kill them and Hermione. As the novel and the series progress, Rowling heightens tension by putting Harry in increasingly dangerous situations.

CHAPTER ELEVEN
Quidditch

Harry's first Quidditch match approaches. One day, in the cold courtyard, Hermione conjures a fire to warm herself, Harry, and Ron. Snape limps toward the students, who are sure he will spot the fire and punish them for it. Instead, Snape confiscates the book Harry is holding, *Quidditch Through the Ages*, and takes five points from Gryffindor, saying that Harry should not have library books outside the school building.

Harry goes to the staff room in search of his book. He opens the door and sees Filch helping Snape wrap bandages around his badly injured leg. Snape is saying he could not watch all three heads at once. He spots Harry and screams at him to get out. Harry tells Ron and Hermione that Snape wants to steal whatever the dog is guarding and must have let in the troll to distract the rest of the school.

The day of the Quidditch match arrives. Hagrid sits with Ron, Hermione, and Neville. As Harry plays, he suddenly loses control of his broom, which climbs into the air and nearly throws him off. Harry holds on by one hand. Hermione spots Snape staring at Harry and muttering. Surmising that Snape is jinxing Harry's broom, she sneaks up to him, knocking over Quirrell in the process, and sets fire to his robe. The fire distracts Snape, and Harry regains control of the broom. He dives toward the ground and manages to catch the Golden Snitch in his mouth, winning the match for Gryffindor.

At tea after the match, Harry, Ron, and Hermione tell Hagrid that Snape tried to kill Harry. Hagrid insists that Snape would never do such a thing. Harry tells Hagrid what he found out about Snape and the three-headed dog. Hagrid, shocked that the children know about the dog, admits that **Fluffy** belongs to him. He lets it slip that what Fluffy is guarding has to do with Professor Dumbledore and **Nicolas Flamel**.

FLUFFY THE DOG bears a close resemblance to Cerberus, the canine guardian of the underworld in Greek mythology. Cerberus is a three-headed dog with a snake-headed tail, and a servant of Hades. Rowling jokes about this connection, writing that Hagrid bought Fluffy from "a Greek chappie."

Chapter Eleven

Clues and Red Herrings: Rowling situates her characters in the familiar tradition of children's mystery stories, presenting them with a puzzle, clues, and red herrings. After discovering the three-headed dog and its mission, Harry, Ron, and Hermione believe they understand the crime about to be committed. In keeping with mystery conventions, however, they must sift through false clues and eliminate likely suspects before they can identify the true villain. Rowling sets up several possible solutions to the mystery, hinting at the real one in a seemingly insignificant sentence.

Two Teams Emerge: Quidditch, which pits the noble, kind students of Gryffindor against the obnoxious, snobby Slytherin students, stands for the larger clash of good and evil at Hogwarts. Like the Quidditch teams, Hogwarts is divided into two sides: those who support Dumbledore and the spirit of Hogwarts, and those who seem to be plotting against the school. Harry's success at Quidditch foreshadows the success he will find in a more important standoff between good and evil. Harry does not work alone, however. His Quidditch teammates help him, and so does Hermione. By going after Snape, she helps Harry win the Quidditch match and probably saves him from falling off the broom to his death. Rowling places great importance on Quidditch because, like life at Hogwarts, it demands individual talent and teamwork in equal measure.

SCHOOL GAMES

To past or current students at British boarding schools, Quidditch will seem familiar, for it is a near cousin to games commonly played at those institutions. Rugby, for instance, was invented at Rugby School in the 1820s. Eton is well known for its game of Fives, a version of handball first played against the side of the school chapel in the early nineteenth century.

CHAPTER TWELVE
The Mirror of Erised

Harry signs up to stay at Hogwarts during Christmas vacation. The Weasleys will stay too. Malfoy teases Harry about not having a real family and insults Ron's family. Ron grabs Malfoy's robes, causing Snape to take five points from Gryffindor.

Harry, Ron, and Hermione tell Hagrid they have been looking in the library for information on Nicolas Flamel. Hagrid tells them to call off the search, but the children continue to hunt for clues in the library. Harry loiters near the Restricted Section, wondering if the elusive information they seek is there, but **Madam Pince**, the librarian, chases him off.

During the holidays, Ron teaches Harry to play wizard chess using live pieces. On Christmas morning, Harry receives a wooden flute from Hagrid, a sweater from Mrs. Weasley, a fifty-pence piece from the Dursleys, and a box of Chocolate Frogs from Hermione. He opens another package and finds an invisibility cloak. An unsigned note in the package says the cloak belonged to his father. The children eat a sumptuous Christmas dinner in the Great Hall, which is decorated with a dozen huge Christmas trees.

That night, Harry puts on his invisibility cloak and ventures into the Restricted Section of the library. One of the books screams when he opens it, so Harry leaves quickly. He manages to sneak past Filch, who cannot see him, but Filch goes to Snape and reports that someone has been in the Restricted Section. Harry hides from Filch and Snape in an unfamiliar classroom. The room contains a giant mirror in which Harry sees a crowd of people surrounding him. He gradually realizes that the people are his family members. He recognizes two of them as his parents. Harry and his parents can wave to each other but cannot talk. After looking at them for a long time, Harry leaves.

The next night, Harry returns with Ron in tow. Ron sees not Harry's family, but himself depicted as Head Boy and captain of the Quidditch team. The next day, Ron tells Harry not to return to the mirror, but Harry ignores him. When he returns to the classroom, he finds Dumbledore, who explains to Harry that the Mirror of Erised shows the "most desperate desires of our hearts." Harry wishes to see his family, so he sees his family. Ron wishes to outshine his brothers, so he sees himself glorified. Dumbledore says that the mirror will be moved the next day and cautions Harry against looking for it again.

UNDERSTANDING AND INTERPRETING
Chapter Twelve

Three Families: Neither Harry nor Ron come from picture-perfect families complete with happy parents, social status, and plenty of money. Occasionally, they suffer because of their families. Harry, an orphan unwanted by his relatives, must endure Malfoy's barbs. Ron, a poor boy with a rat instead of an owl, must tolerate the embarrassments of his family's poverty. However, neither boy is undone by his imperfect background. Harry is kinder and smarter than Malfoy, despite growing up without parents. Ron's family is tightly knit and happy despite its poverty. And both boys begin to form a new family with Hermione and Hagrid.

Discovering Desire: Harry's discovery of the mirror of Erised develops the plot and reveals more about Harry's own character. Symbolically, the mirror is a mirror into the viewer's soul, depicting the viewer's deepest desire. Harry stumbles upon the mirror while investigating the mysterious Nicolas Flamel, and while the mirror tells him nothing about Flamel, it does tell him how fiercely he longs for his parents. Like the invisibility cloak, the mirror of Erised helps Harry connect his present adventures with the past world of his parents. Later in the novel, Rowling will show us the crucial importance of Harry's love for his parents. The turn from the outer world of library research to the inner world of memories and desires suggests that Harry should seek answers not only from the world, but from himself. The discovery of the mirror is also important because it prompts the first intimate, friendly conversation between Harry and Dumbledore.

ERISED DESIRE

Although Dumbledore explains the Mirror of Erised to Harry, he does not translate the mirror's inscription, "Erised stra ehru oyt ube cafru oyt on wohsi.". Readers may realize that because these words speak for a mirror, they should be reversed, just as mirror-writing must be held up to the mirror in order to be understood. When reversed, the inscription reads, "I show not your face but your heart's desire.".

CHAPTER THIRTEEN
Nicolas Flamel

Harry learns that Snape will referee the upcoming Quidditch match between Gryffindor and Hufflepuff and worries that Snape might try to kill him. Ron and Hermione encourage Harry not to play, but he says he must. If the Gryffindor house wins, it will take the lead in the race for the house cup. Slytherin has won the house cup competition for six years in a row.

Neville hops into the common room, his legs stuck together by a Leg-Locker Curse Malfoy put on him. Hermione performs the counter-curse and Ron tells Neville he must stand up to Malfoy. On the verge of tears, Neville says that Malfoy told him he is not brave enough for Gryffindor. Harry tells Neville he is worth twelve Malfoys and gives him a Chocolate Frog. Neville gives Harry the trading card, a picture of Dumbledore. On the back of the card,

"I think the book is a marvelous traditional children's story and excellently written. It is also amusing, exciting and wholesome, and is just the sort of story families should be encouraged to read. In the book, goodness, honesty and integrity overcome lies and deceit."

THE VERY REVEREND NICHOLAS BURY,
DEAN OF GLOUCESTER

Harry reads again that Dumbledore's partner in the study of alchemy was Nicolas Flamel. Hermione fetches a large book and reads that Flamel is "the only known maker of the Sorcerer's Stone." The Stone turns any metal into gold and produces an elixir that gives immortality. The children conclude that Fluffy is guarding Flamel's Sorcerer's Stone.

On the day of the Quidditch match, Harry is relieved to hear that Dumbledore is in the stands. He does not think Snape will harm him with Dumbledore watching. Malfoy sits behind Ron, Hermione, and Neville. Malfoy insults Neville, and Neville says, "I'm worth twelve of you." Malfoy comments on Ron's poverty. Ron attacks Malfoy, giving him a black eye, and Neville comes to his aid, taking on Crabbe and Goyle. Within five minutes of the game's commencement, Harry catches the Golden Snitch, winning the match for Gryffindor.

As Harry leaves the locker room, he sees Snape hurrying to the Forbidden Forest. Harry follows on his broomstick, settling in a tree to hear Snape talking

THE SECRET OF THE PHILOSOPHER'S STONE

The science of alchemy, which dates back to ancient China and Egypt, was especially popular during the Middle Ages. Alchemists believed it was possible to bring base metals to the "perfect" level of gold. They also believed in the perfectibility of the human soul, which would prolong life indefinitely. Ancient Chinese alchemists conceived the idea of a "Philosopher's Stone" that could both turn metals into gold and extend life. The original title of Rowling's novel, *Harry Potter and the Philosopher's Stone*, links the ancient study of alchemy and belief in the Stone with the events of Harry's life. As with other elements of the Potter books, such as wizards and dragons, the mythical Philosopher's Stone actually exists in Harry's world.

Rowling's character Nicolas Flamel is named for the real alchemist Nicolas Flamel, who lived in the fourteenth century. As a bookseller in Paris, Flamel acquired an ancient book written in code that he believed explained the secret of the Philosopher's Stone. He claimed, in his writings, that he created gold on three occasions. Flamel eventually became wealthy but lived modestly and endowed many charitable organizations. A book written in the seventeenth century claimed that Flamel was still alive.

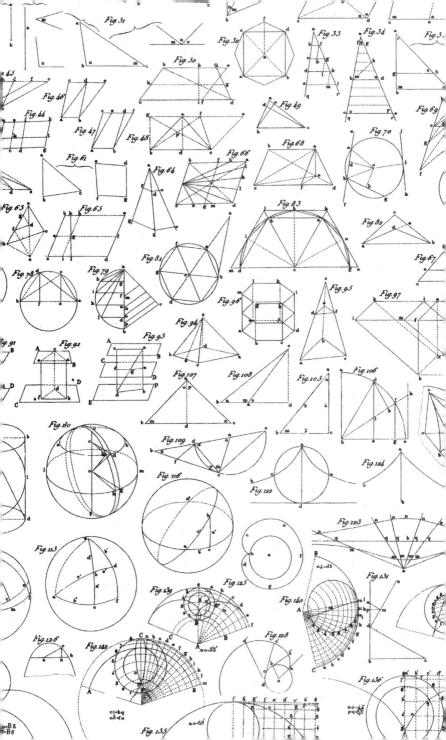

with Quirrell. Snape mentions the Sorcerer's Stone and asks Quirrell if he has found out how to get past the three-headed dog. Snape tells Quirrell, who seems confused, to decide where his "loyalties lie."

Ron and Hermione celebrate the Gryffindor victory, the thrashing of Malfoy, and the bravery of Neville. Harry returns and explains what he saw in the forest. The students conclude that Snape is trying to force Quirrell to help him steal the Sorcerer's Stone.

UNDERSTANDING AND INTERPRETING
Chapter Thirteen

Facing the Bullies: In Chapter Seven, the Sorting Hat proclaimed that Gryffindors are "brave at heart." In Chapter Thirteen, several Gryffindors prove the hat right. Harry insists on playing in the Quidditch match even though he believes that Snape will try to kill him. Neville finally stands up to Malfoy and his henchmen, taking on Crabbe and Goyle. Attacking the two large boys may be tactically unwise, but at least Neville shows the bullies that he has spirit. Ron stands up to Malfoy, blackening his enemy's eye and getting a bloody nose himself. Rowling suggests that sometimes bullies must be faced and fought even if mixed results are the likely outcome.

CHAPTER FOURTEEN
Norbert the Norwegian Ridgeback

The students are swamped with work. Hermione begins preparing for end-of-year exams. One day, Hagrid meets the students in the library. Ron discovers that Hagrid was looking for information on dragons.

Harry, Ron, and Hermione visit Hagrid to get more information about who and what is guarding the Sorcerer's Stone. Hermione flatters Hagrid by emphasizing how much Dumbledore trusts him. Hagrid admits that the Stone is guarded not just by Fluffy, but by spells from Professors **Sprout**, Flitwick, McGonagall, Quirrell, and Snape. The children guess that Snape knows how to disarm all the spells except Quirrell's, which would explain the confrontation in the forest. Hagrid says only he and Dumbledore know "how to get past Fluffy."

Harry complains of the heat in the cabin, and the children notice a dragon's egg in the fire. Hagrid, who won the egg from a stranger in the pub, brushes off the children's warnings about the dangers of hatching a dragon. A few days later, Harry, Ron, and Hermione argue about visiting Hagrid to watch the dragon hatch.

They see Malfoy nearby and worry he has overheard them, but nevertheless they go to Hagrid's hut to see the dragon's birth. Hagrid sees a student peeping in the window. They all rush outside in time to see Malfoy running back to school.

Norbert, the dragon, grows quickly and bites Ron's hand. Worried, the children decide to write to Charlie Weasley, who is studying dragons in Romania. Charlie responds, saying he will take the dragon to Romania. Some friends of his will pick it up from Hogwarts's tallest tower at midnight on Saturday. Malfoy borrows a book from Ron, and Ron belatedly realizes he left Charlie's letter in the book.

Harry and Hermione use the invisibility cloak to sneak out to Hagrid's hut and fetch Norbert, whom Hagrid has put into a crate for the journey. They carry him up to the highest tower but stop when they see Malfoy and McGonagall ahead of them. McGonagall has caught Malfoy, who was lying in wait for Harry and Hermione. She gives him detention and takes twenty points from Slytherin. After she leaves, Harry and Hermione continue up and successfully give the dragon to Charlie's friends. They forget the invisibility cloak at the top of the tower, and Filch catches them as they make their way down.

UNDERSTANDING AND INTERPRETING
Chapter Fourteen

Foolish Optimism: As Harry learns about the mystery of the Sorcerer's Stone, we learn about Hagrid's character. Hagrid is more simple and childlike than Harry and the other students. Love and loyalty define his character—specifically, his love for animals and his loyalty to Dumbledore. Hagrid finds it easy to love fierce creatures, as he demonstrates by nursing a dangerous dragon and naming a murderous three-headed dog Fluffy. For Hagrid, even wild and monstrous nature is full of kindness. Hagrid's affection for violent beasts reveals his inability to think badly of any animal or human. This naive optimism leaves him ill-equipped to fathom the villainous plots afoot at Hogwarts, since he cannot imagine anyone wanting to unseat the beloved Dumbledore. Hagrid's optimism is not just charming; it is foolish. In insisting on seeing only the sunny side of life, Hagrid demonstrates the uselessness of naiveté in the face of clever villains. Harry shares some of Hagrid's innocence and suffers for it. Rowling suggests it is unwise to help your friends indiscriminately, and it is not immoral to think of your self-interest before rescuing other people's dragons.

Junior Villain: Although Harry and his friends suspect Snape of wrongdoing, they do not have firm evidence against him. In the absence of a confirmed villain, Malfoy makes a serviceable bad guy for the characters to hate and the readers to root against. Many young readers will enjoy booing Malfoy and watching him get his comeuppance from Ron and from Hogwarts teachers, especially because Malfoy is the textbook schoolyard bully familiar to most students. Malfoy provokes continual ire because Harry never quite gets the better of him. Harry enjoys triumphs on the Quidditch field, but Malfoy continues his merciless taunting and manages to escape serious punishment.

CHAPTER FIFTEEN
The Forbidden Forest

Filch takes Harry and Hermione to McGonagall's office. McGonagall arrives with Neville, who has been caught trying to warn the others about Malfoy. McGonagall gives them all detention and takes 150 points from Gryffindor, putting Gryffindor in last place for the house cup. Most of the school is furious with Harry, who decides to stop "sneaking around and spying."

One day, Harry hears Quirrell in a classroom saying, "not again," and then sobbing, "all right." He assumes that Snape has finally convinced Quirrell to help him steal the Sorcerer's Stone. Hermione suggests telling Dumbledore, but Harry doubts the Headmaster would believe their word against Snape's. Harry, Hermione, and Neville receive notes telling them their detention will be served that night. Filch takes them and Malfoy to Hagrid, who says they will be going into the Forbidden Forest. Malfoy refuses until Hagrid tells him that his only other option is expulsion. Hagrid shows them unicorn blood on the ground and explains that for the second time in a week, something has attacked a unicorn. They must try to find out what caused it.

They split into two groups. Malfoy goes with Neville and Fang, and Harry and Hermione go with Hagrid. Hagrid hears something slithering past and makes Harry and Hermione hide. They meet two centaurs, **Ronan** and **Bane**, but Hagrid cannot get any information out of them. The centaurs will only discuss the night sky. Hermione sees red sparks, the agreed-upon distress signal for the search parties. Hagrid runs off to help and returns with Neville and Malfoy. Malfoy grabbed Neville to scare him, and Neville set off sparks. Hagrid sends Harry with Malfoy, since Harry will not frighten as easily as Neville.

Harry sees more unicorn blood on the ground, and the boys arrive at a clearing where a dead unicorn lies. A figure in a hood crawls to the unicorn and drinks its blood. Malfoy screams and runs away. Harry feels pain in his scar. Another centaur arrives, and the hooded figure leaves. The centaur, **Firenze**, recognizes

Harry and offers to carry him. Ronan and Bane arrive, and Bane criticizes Firenze for carrying a human, saying he cannot change what the stars foretell.

Firenze explains that drinking unicorn blood gives you life, but it is cursed life. Unicorn blood would be perfect for someone who only needed to stay alive until he could drink some other, more powerful potion. Harry remembers the Sorcerer's Stone, and, with some prompting from Firenze, realizes the mysterious figure must be Voldemort. When he returns to the common room, he tells Ron and Hermione that Snape is trying to steal the Stone for Voldemort, and once he does, Voldemort will kill Harry. Hermione says that Harry will be safe as long as Dumbledore is near. In bed, Harry finds the invisibility cloak under his sheets with a note that reads, "Just in case."

UNDERSTANDING AND INTERPRETING
Chapter Fifteen

Cowardice and Bravery: In Chapter Fifteen, Rowling puts Harry and Malfoy in identical straits in order to highlight the difference between them. The two boys committed the same infraction and received the same punishment. They must go to the same forest and face the same evil. Malfoy, fearful, refuses to go into the Forbidden Forest until threatened with expulsion. His façade of toughness masks his cowardice. He is cast as the stereotypical rich boy, spineless and weak-willed underneath his money. In contrast, Harry shows no real signs of fear. He worries more about the opinion of his peers, who are angry with him for hurting Gryffindor's chances, than about the prospect of physical danger. Malfoy again displays his cowardice when he runs screaming from the hooded figure. Although Voldemort poses a greater risk to Harry than to Malfoy, Harry stands his ground while Malfoy flees.

Flight of Death: The spectacle of the dying unicorn shocks not only because it is the novel's first depiction of death, but because the unicorn symbolizes innocence and purity. When it is murdered, we see death not as a natural step in the cycle of life, but as an unnatural, violent end. Voldemort steals the unicorn's life. It is no coincidence that "Vol de mort" means either "flight of death" or "theft of death" in French. Both names fit his crime. Voldemort is a force of death, and the unicorn's life is stolen by death. Harry is the only witness to Voldemort's violence, as he was when Voldemort murdered his parents. In both Eastern and Western mythology, the unicorn often symbolizes pure, selfless womanhood. Voldemort's murder of the unicorn echoes his murder of Harry's mother, a woman who died selflessly while protecting her baby.

THE TALE OF BARRY TROTTER

In July 2002, Simon & Schuster published a novel by Michael Gerber called *Barry Trotter and the Unauthorized Parody*. Before landing his book with Simon & Schuster, Gerber shopped his manuscript around to several publishers, and self-published it after meeting with rejection. His parody features a twenty-two-year-old named Barry and his friends Ermine Cringer and Lon Measly. The trio defend Hogwash school against Lord Valumart. Gerber calls the book "a dig at Warner Brothers' enormous marketing campaign" for the first *Harry Potter* film.

CHAPTER SIXTEEN
Through the Trapdoor

The students finish their exams. Harry tells Ron and Hermione that his scar has been hurting and then announces suddenly that they must see Hagrid. The children ask Hagrid how he won the egg. He admits he talked to a hooded stranger about odd animals and told this stranger that Fluffy could be calmed by music.

The students rush to Dumbledore to give him this information, but McGonagall tells them that Dumbledore has just left for the Ministry of Magic. They tell McGonagall someone is going to steal the Sorcerer's Stone. She is surprised that they know about the Stone but assures them it is well-guarded. Snape warns Harry that expulsion will result if he is caught outside the dormitory at night again. In the common room, Harry announces he will steal the Stone that night. The danger of Voldemort's return is more important than the risk of expulsion. Ron and Hermione vow to go with him.

When Neville tries to stop them from leaving, Hermione casts a full Body-Bind spell on him, leaving him immobile on the floor. Harry, who is wearing the invisibility cloak, outwits Peeves by pretending to be the **Bloody Baron**, the Slytherin ghost and the only being at Hogwarts who scares Peeves. The children find the door of the third-floor corridor open and realize that someone is ahead of them.

Harry plays Hagrid's flute to lull Fluffy to sleep. They open the trap door and drop into darkness, landing on something soft. It is a large plant, which quickly binds them in its tendrils and refuses to let go. Hermione recognizes the plant as Devil's Snare, a growth that abhors light. She makes a fire with her wand and frees herself and the boys.

They enter a chamber filled with sparkling birds. They cannot pass through the chamber because its door is locked. They realize that the birds are keys, and they must fly on their broomsticks and capture the right one. Using his Seeker skills, Harry captures the key with help from the others. They unlock the door and walk into a room containing a huge chessboard with living figures. They must play their way across the room. Ron directs the chess match, and all three act as pieces. Each time a piece is taken, its opponent violently smashes it. Ron sacrifices himself so Harry can put the king in checkmate. Harry and Hermione advance to the next chamber, reluctantly leaving Ron unconscious on the chessboard.

READING MORE ROWLING

In 2001, Rowling issued two slim paperback volumes, *Quidditch Through the Ages*, by Kennilworthy Whisp, and *Fantastic Beasts and Where to Find Them*, by Newt Scamander. Both books are mentioned in *Harry Potter and the Sorcerer's Stone*. The former is confiscated by Snape in Chapter Eleven, and the latter is on the list of required books in Chapter Five. Rowling donated the proceeds of the sale of these books to Comic Relief U.K., a worldwide organization to help needy children.

They find a troll lying on the floor of the next room, defeated by whomever is ahead of them. In the next chamber, they encounter flames. In order to pass through the fire, they must use four clues to decide which one of seven bottles will help them pass through the flames. Hermione solves the puzzle, but there is only a single swallow of liquid left in the bottle. Harry makes Hermione drink from another bottle, which will allow her to pass backwards. He tells her to retrieve Ron and use the broomsticks in the flying-key chamber to take a message to Dumbledore. She hugs him and commends his bravery, then drinks and disappears through the flames. Harry drinks and goes to the next chamber, where someone is waiting.

UNDERSTANDING AND INTERPRETING
Chapter Sixteen

Sacrifice and Nobility: In an impassioned speech, Harry declares his willingness to suffer expulsion if it means he can get to the Sorcerer's Stone before Voldemort steals it, proving that he is less concerned for his own safety than for the safety of his world. He tells Hermione, "If Snape gets ahold of the Stone, Voldemort's coming back! . . . There won't be any Hogwarts to get expelled from! He'll flatten it, or turn it into a school for the Dark Arts!" Hermione is a brilliant student, but she lacks Harry's ability to see the big picture and fails to grasp the implications of the Sorcerer's Stone. Harry understands that, compared to the threat posed by Voldemort, the house competition is trivial. For all of Harry's bravery, it is Ron who makes the greatest sacrifice in this chapter. In the chess game, Ron symbolically lays down his life for his friends. Their willingness to sacrifice themselves makes Harry, Ron, and Hermione noble.

CHAPTER SEVENTEEN
The Man With Two Faces

To Harry's shock, it is Quirrell he sees in the room. Quirrell says it was he who tried to kill Harry at the Quidditch match. Snape was trying to save Harry with a countercurse. Quirrell says he will kill Harry tonight, and Harry suddenly finds himself bound with rope. He notices that the Mirror of Erised is in the room. Quirrell says that Snape has been trying to stop him. Snape hates Harry, Quirrell claims, because he hated James Potter when they were students together. Quirrell admits he tried to steal the Stone from Gringotts.

RED-BLOODED AND
SHAMELESS

The motion picture *Harry Potter and the Sorcerer's Stone* was released by Warner Brothers on November 16, 2001. Roger Ebert called the film a "red-blooded adventure movie, dripping with atmosphere, filled with the gruesome and the sublime, and surprisingly faithful to the novel." *Salon* called it "a big and often sloppy Hollywood production with . . . bad computer graphics." The *New York Times* called it "dreary, literal-minded," and "shameless." The film grossed over $90 million in its first weekend of release.

Quirrell asks for help from his master, and Harry hears a voice say, "Use the boy." Quirrell makes Harry look in the mirror. Harry realizes that because it is his deepest desire to find the Stone, the mirror will show him finding it. Indeed, when he looks in the mirror, he sees that the Stone is in his own pocket. He tells Quirrell that he sees himself winning the house cup. The voice accuses Harry of lying, and Quirrell unwraps his turban to reveal a second face on the back of his head—the face of Voldemort, who has been sharing Quirrell's body. Voldemort asks for the contents of Harry's pocket, but Harry refuses. Voldemort says that Harry's mother only

> "Ms. Rowling's books cannibalize and synthesize pop culture mythology, proof of the nothing-will-ever-go-away ethic. She has come up with something like *Star Wars* for a generation that never had a chance to thrill to its grandeur, but this is *Young Sherlock Holmes* as written by C.S. Lewis from a story by Roald Dahl."
>
> **ELVIS MITCHELL**, *THE NEW YORK TIMES*

died to protect him. Quirrell grabs Harry, and Harry feels horrible pain in his scar. When Quirrell lets go, he too is in pain, the skin of his fingers blistering. Voldemort commands Quirrell to seize Harry once more. Quirrell does, and again reels back in pain. Harry realizes his touch hurts Quirrell and puts his hands on Quirrell's face. He holds fast to Quirrell, but at last his own pain causes Harry to black out.

When Harry regains consciousness, Dumbledore is standing over him. Harry starts telling Dumbledore that Quirrell has the stone, but Dumbledore tells him to relax. Harry realizes he is in the hospital. He asks Dumbledore again about the Stone, and Dumbledore tells him he arrived just in time to save Harry from Quirrell. He and Nicolas Flamel decided that the Sorcerer's Stone must be destroyed. When Harry asks if Nicolas Flamel will die, Dumbledore says, "Death is but the next great adventure." He tells Harry that his mother's love protected Harry, warding off Quirrell. Dumbledore admits to giving the invisibility cloak to Harry but will not explain why Voldemort wanted to kill him when he was a baby. He says James Potter saved Snape's life, and Snape had to protect Harry so he could go back to hating James. Finally, Dumbledore reveals that the mirror was enchanted in such a way that only someone who wanted to find the Stone without using it would discover it.

x

J. K. Rowling

Ron and Hermione visit Harry in the hospital wing. So does Hagrid, who brings a present—an album filled with wizard photographs of Harry's parents. At the end-of-year feast, it appears that Slytherin will win the house cup again. But Dumbledore awards points to Harry, Ron, and Hermione for their brave actions. Gryffindor and Slytherin are tied for first place. Dumbledore then awards ten points to Neville for standing up to his friends. Gryffindor wins the cup.

The students pack up and board the Hogwarts Express for London, where the Dursleys meet Harry. Harry looks forward to keeping his magic current by practicing on Dudley.

UNDERSTANDING AND INTERPRETING
Chapter Seventeen

The Power of Love: The previous chapters lauded character traits such as courage, sacrifice, and loyalty. In the final chapter, love emerges as the most useful quality in combating evil. Harry does not understand the strength of love until he awakes in the hospital wing and Dumbledore explains what made him able to withstand Quirrell's and Voldemort's violence. The greatest lesson learned throughout this adventure may be that love for others is more valuable than the pursuit of one's own desires, which is really nothing more than love for one's self.

The Danger of Power: Rowling suggests that it is acceptable to cultivate power only if you behave responsibly once you have it. Dumbledore has exceptional power, but he uses it wisely. He shows the students that although Slytherin house acquired a lot of points, victory should go to the house that has engaged in a just and righteous struggle. Flamel must destroy the Sorcerer's Stone because its power is so great it tempts people to great evil. Power is important, but morality is more important.

Mysteries Solved and Unsolved: The final chapter of a mystery novel traditionally answers questions and wraps up loose ends. Quirrell and Dumbledore explain many of the mysteries that have been troubling Harry, but as befits the first volume in a series, many mysteries remain unanswered, from mundane matters such as who will take over as the Defense Against the Dark Arts teacher, to more important ones, such as how James Potter saved Snape's life, why Harry's scar sometimes pains him, how Voldemort will return, and why Voldemort tried and failed to kill Harry years ago. These questions encourage readers to buy the next novel in the series.

Conclusions

While Rowling draws on the tradition of the boarding school novel, she is most influenced by fantasy novels such as Tolkien's *The Lord of the Rings*, which itself drew heavily on Greek mythology and Christianity. In both Rowling's and Tolkien's series, a kindly wizard (Gandalf, Dumbledore) entrusts a small group of short people (Hobbits, Hogwarts students) with essential tasks in defeating a dark lord (Sauron, Voldemort). Both dark lords have suffered defeats that resulted in the loss of their physical bodies. Their influence has been absent from the world for a time, but they are trying to regain their power. Both search for objects (the One Ring, the Sorcerer's Stone) that they will use to launch campaigns to return to full power.

The Harry Potter novels fit into many literary genres, but some readers see them as most similar to fairy tales. The Dursleys are reminiscent of Cinderella's evil step-family, and like Cinderella, Harry receives magical help in escaping from them. In an article in *The New Yorker*, Joan Acocella points out that Rowling follows many of the conventions of the fairy tale, as outlined in Vladimir Propp's 1928 book *Morphology of the Folk Tale*. Propp explains that in fairy tales, a villain harms a member of the hero's family; the hero is branded, banished, and released; the hero undergoes difficult ordeals and requires help from wise advisors; the villain changes his form; and at last the hero marries. With the exception of marriage, *Harry Potter and the Sorcerer's Stone* follows this progression precisely. Voldemort kills Harry's parents and brands Harry with a scar. Harry is banished to the Dursleys and released to Hogwarts, where Dumbledore and others aid him. Voldemort changes shape, becoming a face on the back of Quirrell's head. Rowling repeats this pattern in subsequent volumes in the series, with Harry beginning each volume in exile at the Dursleys and ending each volume by encountering Voldemort (or his servant) in a new form.

III

HARRY POTTER AND THE CHAMBER OF SECRETS

Key Facts

Genre: Children's fantasy novel, bildungsroman (coming-of-age novel); the second in a planned series of seven novels

Date of First Publication: 1999

Setting: Modern-day England. London and Hogwarts School of Witchcraft and Wizardry

Narrator: Anonymous, third-person observer

Plot Overview: Harry Potter returns to Hogwarts, where he encounters the new Defense Against the Dark Arts teacher, a smarmy but good-looking author named Gilderoy Lockhart. Hogwarts suffers a series of attacks. Harry finds the enchanted diary of Tom Riddle, who attended Hogwarts fifty years earlier. Lucius Malfoy arranges Hagrid's arrest and Dumbledore's suspension. Harry and Ron find the entrance to the Chamber of Secrets, where Harry faces and defeats the Basilisk, a giant snake with a deadly stare, and Tom Riddle, the youthful incarnation of Lord Voldemort, who has been causing the attacks. Dumbledore returns to school and praises the boys.

Style, Technique, and Language

Style and Technique—Nearly Normal: The narrator describes the events of Hogwarts as if they are perfectly normal. Indeed, most *are* perfectly normal. Harry, Hermione, and Ron experience nearly everything exactly as normal boarding school students do, from their dining hall meals to their teachers' personalities. Magic is a restricted, safe element in their otherwise ordinary lives. They learn magic in the same bland, dogged way in which other students learn algebra.

The ordinariness of Harry and his friends makes it easy for school children to relate to them. Like most students, Harry has friends and enemies, struggles with his homework load, likes some teachers and hates others, and gets in trouble for breaking school rules.

Language—Living Latin: Rowling sprinkles Latin throughout the Harry Potter series, giving a vaguely medieval air to the education at Hogwarts. Harry learns spells in Latin. "Lumos" is Latin for "light," for example, and "expelliarmus" derives from the Latin for "to expel a weapon." In the Middle Ages, scholars used Latin, and most books were written in Latin. Along with the setting and architecture of Hogwarts, which suggest the Middle Ages, the use of Latin gives us the feeling that Hogwarts exists in another time. In an online interview, Rowling discussed her use of Latin in the novels, saying, "I like to think that the wizards use this dead language as a living language." She also pointed out that the use of Latin provides clues for the readers.

Characters in *Harry Potter and the Chamber of Secrets*

Aragog: A giant spider hatched and raised by Hagrid fifty years ago. Hagrid treats the spider kindly, even finding him a mate, but Aragog remains murderous.

The Basilisk: A giant snake placed in the Chamber of Secrets by Salazar Slytherin and released fifty years ago by Tom Riddle. Working under the influence of Riddle's diary, Ginny Weasley releases the Basilisk, which can kill by looking into its victim's eyes.

Professor Binns: A ghost who teaches the History of Magic. Hermione persuades him to tell the legend of the Chamber of Secrets.

Mr. Borgin: The proprietor of a shop in Knockturn Alley that deals in supplies for the Dark Arts.

The Bloody Baron: A Slytherin ghost.

Lavender Brown: A student at Hogwarts.

Milicent Bulstrode: A large Slytherin girl who fights with Hermione at the Dueling Club.

Penelope Clearwater: A Ravenclaw prefect who is a victim of the same attack that Petrifies Hermione. Penelope dates Percy Weasley.

Crabbe: One of Draco Malfoy's dimwitted cronies. Ron takes on Crabbe's appearance when he drinks the Polyjuice Potion.

Colin Creevey: A Gryffindor first-year and a huge fan of Harry's. Colin's hobby is photography.

Sir Patrick Delaney-Podmore: The leader of the Headless Hunt. He excludes Nearly Headless Nick but comes to Nick's deathday party.

Armando Dippet: The Headmaster of Hogwarts when the Chamber of Secrets was first opened.

Dobby: Lucius Malfoy's house-elf. Dobby warns Harry not to return to Hogwarts. Humble Dobby is prone to masochism.

Albus Dumbledore: The Headmaster of Hogwarts. Lucius Malfoy conspires to get Dumbledore suspended from his job, but Dumbledore still manages to help Harry in the battle against the Basilisk. Dumbledore eventually returns to Hogwarts at the insistence of the school's governors.

Dudley Dursley: The corpulent cousin of Harry Potter. Dudley teases Harry about having no friends at his "freak" school.

Petunia Dursley: Harry's aunt. Mrs. Dursley punishes Harry by making him do hours of hard manual labor. She tries to host a perfect dinner party for her husband's client, Mr. Mason.

Vernon Dursley: Harry's uncle. Mr. Dursley hates Harry and any mention of magic. A seller of drills, he hopes to land a major account with Mr. Mason.

Errol: An old, decrepit owl that belongs to the Weasleys.

Fang: Hagrid's dog.

The Fat Friar: A Hufflepuff ghost.

Fawkes: Dumbledore's pet phoenix. Like all phoenixes, he can carry heavy loads and heal wounds with his tears. Fawkes helps Harry defeat the Basilisk in the Chamber of Secrets.

> "The five years I spent on *Harry Potter and the Philosopher's Stone* were spent constructing The Rules. I had to lay down all my parameters. The most important thing to decide when you're creating a fantasy world is what the characters can't do."
>
> J.K. ROWLING

Argus Filch: The caretaker at Hogwarts. Filch delights in catching students in the act of misbehaving. Harry discovers that Filch is a Squib —someone born of magical parents but lacking magical abilities himself.

Seamus Finnigan: A second-year in Gryffindor who sleeps in Harry's dormitory.

Justin Finch-Fletchley: A Hufflepuff student with Muggle parents who suspects that Harry is out to get him. Justin is the third victim of a Petrifying attack.

Marcus Flint: The captain of the Slytherin Quidditch team. Flint allows Draco Malfoy to become Seeker after Malfoy's father bribes him with new racing brooms for the team.

Professor Flitwick: The Charms teacher at Hogwarts.

Cornelius Fudge: The Minister of Magic. Cornelius incarcerates Hagrid to make it seem like he has taken disciplinary action.

Goyle: One of Draco Malfoy's dimwitted cronies. Harry takes on Goyle's appearance when he drinks the Polyjuice Potion.

Hermione Granger: A brilliant student and a close friend of Harry. Hermione gets the best grades in her class and takes all possible courses in her third year. She deduces that the beast in the Chamber is a Basilisk, but she is Petrified before she can tell Harry and Ron.

Mr. and Mrs. Granger: Hermione's Muggle parents. Arthur Weasley enjoys talking to them in Diagon Alley.

Godric Gryffindor: One of the four founders of Hogwarts. Gryffindor had a "serious argument" with fellow founder Salazar Slytherin, who wanted to deny admittance to students not born of wizard parents.

Hagrid: The gamekeeper at Hogwarts. Hagrid was expelled from Hogwarts fifty years ago on the false testimony of Tom Riddle, who claimed that Hagrid's pet spider was the creature from the Chamber. Under suspicion of opening the Chamber, Hagrid is sent to Azkaban by Cornelius Fudge.

Hermes: Percy Weasley's owl.

Hedwig: Harry's owl.

Madam Hooch: The Quidditch coach.

Malfada Hopkirk: An official at the Improper Use of Magic Office. Malfada sends a warning letter to Harry.

Olive Hornby: A girl who teased Moaning Myrtle about her glasses fifty years ago.

Helga Hufflepuff: One of the four founders of Hogwarts.

Lee Jordan: A Hogwarts student and a friend of Fred and George Weasley. Lee is the announcer for the Quidditch matches.

"My trepidation over the Harry Potter series is founded on the disconnect between what the books attempt to say . . . and how Rowling says them, a disconnect between form and content. . . . On aesthetic grounds the series is fundamentally failed fantasy. [Rowling] violates the integral rules of the fantasy game, never capturing the integrity of the very fantasy tradition that she is mining for riches."

JOHN PENNINGTON, "THE LION AND THE UNICORN"

Gilderoy Lockhart: A famous author and the new teacher of Defense Against the Dark Arts. Lockhart has a slick style, a huge ego, and a taste for publicity. A complete fraud, he claims as his own the adventures he reads about in books. Lockhart tries to use Ron's broken wand to cast a Memory Charm on Harry and Ron, but the wand backfires and erases Lockhart's memory.

Neville Longbottom: An accident-prone second-year in Gryffindor who sleeps in Harry's dormitory.

Ernie Macmillan: A Hufflepuff student who thinks that Harry is the Heir of Slytherin and a Dark wizard. He apologizes to Harry after Hermione is attacked.

J. K. Rowling

Draco Malfoy: Harry's nemesis at Hogwarts. Malfoy wants to rid Hogwarts of "Mudbloods," those who are not pure-blooded wizards. The attacks please him, as does the exile of Dumbledore.

Lucius Malfoy: Draco's father. Lucius believes in the superiority of pure-blooded wizards and dislikes Muggles. He gives Ginny Weasley Tom Riddle's diary in an attempt to discredit the Weasley family and rid Hogwarts of half-Muggles. He scares the other governors of Hogwarts into suspending Dumbledore, but he eventually loses his position as governor.

Mr. Mason: A potential buyer of Mr. Dursley's drills. Mr. Mason comes to dinner at the Dursleys's house on the night Dobby arrives at the house.

Mrs. Mason: A dinner guest at the Dursleys' home. She is afraid of birds and leaves the house after an owl arrives with a letter for Harry.

Minerva McGonagall: The Transfiguration teacher at Hogwarts and the Head of Gryffindor house. McGonagall takes charge in Dumbledore's absence. A stickler for rules, McGonagall takes the safety of the students very seriously.

Moaning Myrtle: A whiny young ghost who inhabits a toilet in a girls' bathroom. She was killed fifty years ago by a Basilisk.

Nearly Headless Nick: A Gryffindor ghost. Nick gets depressed when Delaney-Podmore excludes him from the Headless Hunt. Nick invites Harry to his 500th deathday party.

Mrs. Norris: Filch's cat. The first victim of the Basilisk, Mrs. Norris is found Petrified on Halloween night.

Parvati Patil: A student at Hogwarts.

Peeves: A Hogwarts poltergeist who delights in making trouble.

Perkins: A warlock and Mr. Weasley's sole assistant at the Misuse of Muggle Artifacts Office.

Madam Pince: The librarian at Hogwarts.

Madam Pomfrey: The nurse at Hogwarts. Lockhart's bungled attempt to fix Harry's broken arm upsets her.

Harry Potter: The twelve-year-old wizard protagonist of the novel. Harry discovers he can speak Parseltongue, the language of snakes. With Ron and Hermione, he tries to ferret out the Heir of Slytherin.

Adrian Pucey: A player on the Slytherin Quidditch team.

Rowena Ravenclaw: One of the four founders of Hogwarts.

Tom Riddle: Perhaps the brightest student ever to attend Hogwarts. Riddle eventually became Lord Voldemort. As a teenager, he kept a diary which now falls into the hands of Ginny Weasley and Harry.

Salazar Slytherin: One of the four founders of Hogwarts. Slytherin wanted to exclude all students born of Muggle parents. He left the school after an argument with Godric Gryffindor on the subject. Slytherin created the Chamber of Secrets, which could be opened only by his Heir.

Severus Snape: The Potions master at Hogwarts and the Head of Slytherin house. Snape wants Harry expelled for flying in an enchanted car and suspended from the Quidditch team for not telling Dumbledore everything he knows about the Chamber of Secrets. Snape arranges for Harry and Malfoy to be dueling partners.

The Sorting Hat: A talking, battered wizard's hat that chooses houses for new Hogwarts students. When Harry tries on the Sorting Hat in Dumbledore's office, it says he would have done well in Slytherin. When battling the Basilisk, Harry uses the hat to conjure the sword of Godric Gryffindor.

Alicia Spinnet: A Chaser for the Gryffindor Quidditch team.

Dean Thomas: A second-year in Gryffindor who sleeps in Harry's dormitory.

Voldemort: The Dark Lord whom the infant Harry defeated. Voldemort began life as Tom Riddle, a half-Muggle child raised in a Muggle orphanage. Riddle's memory, made powerful in his diary, tries to kill Harry in the Chamber of Secrets. Harry discovers that some of Voldemort's powers, such as the ability to speak to snakes, passed to him when he first defeated Voldemort.

Arthur Weasley: The Weasley children's father. He works at the Ministry of Magic tracking down and punishing people who illegally enchant Muggle objects.

Bill Weasley: The oldest Weasley brother. Bill works for the Egypt branch of Gringotts, a wizards' bank.

Charlie Weasley: The second Weasley brother. Charlie studies dragons in Romania.

Fred and George Weasley: The Weasley twins. They enjoy all sorts practical jokes, fireworks, and general rule-breaking. Fred and George are Beaters for the Gryffindor Quidditch team.

Ginny Weasley: The youngest Weasley child and a first-year student at Hogwarts. Ginny has a crush on Harry. She discovers Tom Riddle's diary and communicates with the memory of Tom, pouring out all her intimate secrets to him. Riddle gains control of Ginny and makes her open the Chamber of Secrets and set the Basilisk on various people.

Molly Weasley: The mother of the Weasley family. Mrs. Weasley always treats Harry kindly but can be stern with her children and husband when they behave foolishly.

Percy Weasley: A prefect and a stern enforcer of rules at Hogwarts. Percy behaves strangely throughout the novel, either isolating himself in his room or roaming the Hogwarts castle alone.

Ron Weasley: Harry's best friend at Hogwarts. Ron flies an enchanted car to school. He goes with Harry into the Forbidden Forest and down the tunnel leading to the Chamber of Secrets.

Oliver Wood: The captain of the Gryffindor Quidditch team. Wood is committed to hard work, both mentally and physically.

Reading *Harry Potter and the Chamber of Secrets*

CHAPTER ONE

The Worst Birthday

It is breakfast time at the Dursley house. **Harry Potter**'s uncle, **Vernon Dursley**, scolds Harry for letting his pet owl, **Hedwig**, make so much noise. Harry says Hedwig complains because Mr. Dursley will not let her out of her cage. When Harry's cousin, **Dudley**, asks Harry to pass the frying pan, Harry asks for the "magic word." The Dursley family reacts with horror to the mention of magic, even though Harry was referring to the magic word "please."

It is the summer after Harry's first year at Hogwarts, and Harry must spend it with the Dursleys. All his books and wizarding supplies have been locked away.

J. K. Rowling

"It's becoming more of a challenge to keep new readers up to speed with every new Harry book. In the case of *Chamber of Secrets*, matters were relatively straightforward; I tried to introduce information about Harry and his first year at Hogwarts in as natural a way as possible. However, by the time I reach books five and six, this is going to be much harder. It makes me think of 'previously on "ER"' when you have to watch thirty minutes of clips to understand that week's episode."

J.K. ROWLING

He misses school and reflects on his discovery, one year ago, that he is a wizard, the son of parents killed by the Dark wizard, **Voldemort**. Voldemort lost his power trying to kill Harry. Today is Harry's twelfth birthday, but the Dursleys take no notice of it. They are busy planning a dinner party for **Mr. Mason**, one of Mr. Dursley's clients. Harry's job for the evening is to hide quietly in his room.

In the garden, Harry wonders why his best friends **Ron Weasley** and **Hermione Granger** have not sent him any letters this summer. Harry sees two green eyes in the hedge, but they disappear when Dudley arrives and teases him. When Harry frightens Dudley by pretending to use magic, **Mrs. Dursley** makes him work for the rest of the day. She feeds him a meager dinner and sends him to his room before the party starts. Harry is surprised to find someone on his bed.

UNDERSTANDING AND INTERPRETING
Chapter One

Refresher Course: Chapter One brings readers up to speed, reviewing the basic particulars of *Harry Potter and the Sorcerer's Stone*. People who read the first volume in the series have a chance to refresh their memories, and people joining the series in the middle will encounter a novel that stands on its own. Quick recaps are standard in children's series books, including *The Famous Five*, *The Hardy Boys*, and *Sweet Valley Twins*. Rowling's reference to events from the past also emphasizes the passage of time. The reader might finish the first Harry Potter novel and dive right into the second, but Harry has been suffering with the Dursleys for several weeks between the end of *The Sorcerer's Stone* and the beginning of *The Chamber of Secrets*.

Return to the Family: Harry matured quickly at Hogwarts, making friends, discovering hidden talents, and excelling in difficult moments. However, the Dursleys continue to scorn Harry and treat him like a cipher. His resounding success at Hogwarts does not even register with them. Like many boarding school or college students, Harry returns home with expanded horizons and a swollen sense of self-importance, only to find that the people he left behind are exactly the same as they were when he left, and that they do not care about or even notice the changes in their thriving student.

CHAPTER TWO
Dobby's Warning

The small creature in Harry's room has "batlike ears" and huge eyes. He is dressed in an old pillowcase and introduces himself as "**Dobby**, the house-elf." When Harry asks Dobby to sit down, the elf starts to sob, saying no wizard has ever treated him so kindly. Dobby bangs his head against the window, saying he is punishing himself for almost speaking ill of the family he serves. He tells Harry a house-elf must serve the same family until death, unless he is set free.

Dobby praises Harry's greatness and then delivers his message, warning Harry to stay away from Hogwarts because of a plot that will put him in mortal danger. Dobby claims that the plot does not involve Voldemort, but when Harry presses him, Dobby starts beating himself again. Mr. Dursley hears noise and comes upstairs to threaten Harry. Harry hides Dobby in the closet until Vernon leaves.

Dobby admits to confiscating all of Harry's letters from his friends, saying he thought if Harry believed he had no friends, he would not want to return to Hogwarts. Harry won't promise not to return, and Dobby runs downstairs. Harry chases him into the kitchen, where he sees Mrs. Dursley's fancy dessert hovering near the ceiling. When Harry again refuses to stay home from Hogwarts, Dobby lets the pudding smash to the floor and then disappears.

An owl arrives with a letter for Harry, scaring away the Masons and ruining Vernon's business deal. The letter cautions Harry against doing magic outside of school. When the Dursleys discover the ban on magic, they lock Harry in his room, barring the window and saying they will not allow him to return to school. Three days later, in the middle of the night, Harry wakes and sees Ron Weasley outside his window.

DOBBY AND DOBIE

Rowling's character Dobby may be inspired by Dobies, who appear in Northern English folklore. Dobies are similar to brownies (kindly elves that perform good deeds at night), although they are "creature[s] of far less sense and activity" than brownies. Common phrases among people living on the border of England and Scotland in the nineteenth century included "O ye stupid Dobie" and "He's but a senseless Dobie." The character Dobby demonstrates some of the same foolish tendencies as the folkloric Dobie.

UNDERSTANDING AND INTERPRETING
Chapter Two

A Wizard Unmanned: When Dobby drops the dessert and leaves, framing Harry for his misdeed, the resulting chaos shows us the depths of injustice possible in the Dursley household. Harry began the day glumly and ends it despairingly. Outside the relative safety of the wizard world, Harry is impotent. Muggles ignore him, belittle him, and treat him unjustly. Harry cannot escape his aunt, free himself or his owl, or control even the smallest event in his house.

New Perspective: The plight of Dobby lessens the intensity of Harry's self-pity. Harry has been feeling sorry for himself because his friends neglect him and he must spend another four weeks with the horrid Dursleys. In contrast to Harry's plight, Dobby must live with a family so awful he cowers in fear even when miles removed from them. He is enslaved until death to people who have never shown him the small kindness of asking him to sit down. As Harry says, Dobby's situation "makes the Dursleys sound almost human."

CHAPTER THREE
The Burrow

Ron is floating outside Harry's window in an old car. In the front seats sit Ron's twin brothers, **Fred** and **George**. The Weasleys attach a rope to the bars on Harry's window and pull them out. Fred and George climb in the window and pick the lock on the cupboard under the stairs so they can retrieve Harry's school things. They have just finished loading everything in the car when Hedwig screeches, waking Mr. Dursley. Harry goes back inside for Hedwig and then bolts to the car, almost eluding his uncle. Mr. Dursley catches him by the ankle, but the Weasleys pull Harry away. The four boys fly off in the car.

Harry tells the Weasleys about Dobby, and they guess his appearance might be a practical joke engineered by **Draco Malfoy**. Draco's father, **Lucius Malfoy**, was one of the chief supporters of Lord Voldemort, although he withdrew his support as soon as Voldemort fell from power. The Weasleys explain that house-elves typically belong to rich old wizarding families like the Malfoys.

They arrive at the Burrow, a dilapidated house where the Weasleys live. **Mrs. Weasley** lectures the boys about the foolishness of their adventure and invites Harry in for breakfast. **Ginny Weasley**, Ron's little sister, peeps into the room and runs away. Ron says that Ginny has been talking about Harry all summer.

After breakfast, Mrs. Weasley sends the boys to de-gnome the garden. She shows them a book by a good-looking wizard named **Gilderoy Lockhart**, suggesting they consult it for tips on de-gnoming, but the boys manage alone, picking up the small leathery gnomes and spinning them around to make them dizzy.

Mr. Arthur Weasley returns from his job at the Misuse of Muggle Artifacts Office, where he confiscates illegally enchanted Muggle objects. Mrs. Weasley lectures him about enchanting the car to make it fly. Ron takes Harry to his tiny room, which is decorated with memorabilia from the Chudley Cannons Quidditch team. Ron is embarrassed by his family's poverty, but Harry says the Burrow is "the best house I've ever been in."

UNDERSTANDING AND INTERPRETING
Chapter Three

Crossing the Threshold: Chapter Three features the escape/transition scene that occurs, in various forms, in each Harry Potter novel. Harry must escape the clutches of the Dursleys and free himself of the Muggle world in order to get to Hogwarts and the magic world. The difficulty of this transition demonstrates the size of the rift between the two worlds. Mr. Dursley, who is disgusted by the idea of anything magical, does not want Harry to cross the threshold and escape the certainty of Four Privet Drive. He objects partly because he enjoys tormenting Harry and partly because he would rather not acknowledge the existence of magic. Once Harry makes his escape, he feels at home for the first time in the novel. The Weasley children and parents enjoy Harry's company, treating him as a friend and equal. They do not fawn over him as Dobby does, nor do they regard him distrustfully as the Dursleys do.

> "The Harry Potter books are an attempt to recall what Peter Hitchens calls "the world we have lost," a reaction against modern living. . . . Harry Potter might be a wizard, and the only one able to withstand the powers of the evil Lord Voldemort, but Harry Potter is a Tory. A paternalistic One-Nation Tory in the tradition of Harold Macmillan and Iain McLeod, perhaps, but a Tory nevertheless."
>
> **RICHARD ADAMS**, *THE GUARDIAN*

Rich in Love: Ron is ashamed of the poverty in which his family lives, but Harry is delighted by the Burrow and its inhabitants. Harry, who has piles of gold waiting for him at Gringotts, craves the rich family life that Ron enjoys. The Weasleys are the kind of family Harry idealizes. The children tease each other, the parents bicker, and Mrs. Weasley scolds the boys when they behave badly. Love suffuses each of these healthy familial activities. The Weasleys' tiny, rundown house humiliates Ron, but Harry hardly notices it. He is fixated on the unconditional love he encounters at the Weasleys', because he has never had the opportunity, as Ron always has, to take it for granted.

CHAPTER FOUR

At Flourish and Blotts

Harry enjoys his stay with the Weasleys. Ginny, who will start attending Hogwarts in September, gets nervous whenever Harry is around. Letters from Hogwarts arrive, listing new books the students need. The list includes seven expensive volumes by Gilderoy Lockhart. The Weasleys' battered owl, **Errol**, brings a letter from Hermione, who will meet Harry and the Weasleys in Diagon Alley. **Percy Weasley** behaves oddly and stays in his bedroom during most of Harry's visit.

To get to Diagon Alley, Fred sprinkles Floo Powder into the fireplace, walks into the high green flames, shouts out "Diagon Alley," and disappears. Harry tries to use Fred's tactic, but something goes wrong, and he emerges in a dark, evil-looking shop on an unfamiliar street. Harry sees Draco Malfoy and his father, Lucius, coming into the shop, and hides in a cabinet. Draco complains of Harry's popularity, but Lucius cautions against making an enemy of someone regarded as a hero.

"Rowling reveals leftish social prejudices all too typical of the British intelligentsia. Harry's main rival at the school, nasty Draco Malfoy is—two strikes—both rich and aristocratic. Meanwhile, the dysfunctional Dursleys, Harry's ghastly family, are a caricature of the vicious bourgeoisie that would have delighted Vyshinsky. They are contrasted with the poor-but-happy Weasleys."

ANDREW STUTTAFORD, *NATIONAL REVIEW*

Mr. Borgin, the shopkeeper, greets Mr. Malfoy, who wants to sell him some illegal potions to avoid being "embarrassed" by a raid. Mr. Malfoy mentions rumors of a new Muggle Protection Act and calls Mr. Weasley a "flea-bitten, Muggle-loving fool." He berates Draco for earning poorer grades than Hermione, who has no wizard blood in her family. Borgin agrees that "wizard blood is counting for less everywhere." When the Malfoys leave the shop, Harry sneaks out. **Hagrid** finds him and drags him to Diagon Alley. Harry had mistakenly wound up in Knockturn Alley, a street filled with shops devoted to the Dark Arts.

Harry meets Hermione and the Weasleys at Gringotts, where Harry and Mrs. Weasley make withdrawals. They go to the bookstore, Flourish and Blotts, where Gilderoy Lockhart is signing copies of his autobiography. Lockhart spots Harry and forces the boy to pose with him for the *Daily Prophet* photographer. He then announces that he will be the new Defense Against the Dark Arts teacher at Hogwarts. Draco Malfoy teases Harry about his fame, and Lucius Malfoy baits Mr. Weasley, remarking on his poverty and his friendship with Hermione's non-wizard parents. Mr. Weasley attacks Mr. Malfoy, but Hagrid breaks up the fight.

UNDERSTANDING AND INTERPRETING
Chapter Four

A Pair of Villains: The Malfoys suggest a combination of familiar villains, including capitalists, aristocrats, Nazis, and white supremacists. Rowling signals Lucius Malfoy's malevolence by making him a successful, rich businessman, in contrast to Mr. Weasley, whose poverty she equates with goodness. Voicing a Nazi sentiment, Lucius rails against the corruption of pure wizard blood. He calls Arthur Weasley a "Muggle-lover," using a term similar to the one white supremacists used for whites who supported the Civil Rights movement in the American South in the 1960s. Rowling suggests that prejudice does not naturally spring up in children, but is taught to them by their parents. Draco simply spouts the beliefs of his father.

Smarmy Lockhart: In the character of Gilderoy Lockhart, Rowling satirizes the cult of celebrity, pointing out that the public chooses its celebrities for looks and charm, not smarts or talent. The alliterative titles of Lockhart's books (*Magical Me, Holidays with Hags, Wanderings with Werewolves*) imply shallow scholarship, and his fans seem much more interested in him as a personality than as an author. Lockhart carefully monitors his status and massages his fame, cleverly associating himself with Harry's celebrity.

CHAPTER FIVE
The Whomping Willow

Summer vacation ends, and the Weasleys and Harry pack for school. Mr. Weasley has enchanted the interior of his car so all the luggage and children can fit comfortably. They make several false starts, returning to the Burrow for things the children have forgotten, and arrive at the station just a few minutes before the Hogwarts Express is due to leave. All the children except Harry and Ron pass through the barrier onto platform nine and three-quarters. When Harry and Ron try to follow, their carts crash into the barrier. For some reason, the secret passage has closed, and they miss the train.

Ron suggests flying the car to Hogwarts, saying that students are allowed to use magic in an emergency. He pushes a button to make the car invisible, and they take off, but the car quickly turns visible again. To avoid being seen, they fly above the clouds. As they approach Hogwarts, the car begins to falter and finally stalls out. They smash

"The Harry Potter books satirize for children the superficiality of this world, its pretenses and human failures, the narcissism of popular culture, the stupidity and cruelty of the press, the rigidity and fraudulence imbedded in our institutions, particularly the schools, framed by the unrelenting snobbery and elitism of our social world."

RONI NATOV, PROFESSOR OF ENGLISH, BROOKLYN COLLEGE

into a tree on the school grounds, and the limbs of the tree begin battering the car. Just when it looks like the tree will crush them, the car restarts. They back up, and the car throws them and their luggage out onto the lawn, then drives away into the darkness. Ron's wand is broken in the accident.

Professor Snape takes Harry and Ron to his office and refuses to listen to their explanation for their behavior. He shows them the *Daily Prophet*, which has a lead story about Muggles sighting a flying car. Harry realizes they could have landed Mr. Weasley in serious trouble. Snape brings **Professor McGonagall** to his office. Furious, she says they should have sent a letter by owl when they could not get through the barrier. **Dumbledore** arrives. He is deeply disappointed in the boys but does not expel them. McGonagall says they will both receive detention.

GRANDPRÉ'S SOFT GEOMETRY

The British editions of the Harry Potter
books are not illustrated, but the American
editions include illustrated chapter head-
ings by Mary Grandpré, who also created
the artwork for the American dust jackets.
Grandpré is a Minnesota artist who has
illustrated several children's books in addition to *Harry Potter*. She works in pastels
and employs what she calls "soft geometry."

The Sorting Ceremony is over. Ginny has been placed in Gryffindor. McGonagall gives the boys supper in Snape's office. Afterward, they go to Gryffindor tower where they are greeted with a scolding from Hermione, harsh looks from Percy, and applause and congratulations from the other Gryffindors.

UNDERSTANDING AND INTERPRETING
Chapter Five

Rule-Breaker: In *Harry Potter and the Sorcerer's Stone*, Harry broke rules on several occasions, usually with good reason. In breaking the rule against using magic, however, Harry acts thoughtlessly. He does not consider alternatives to flying, such as the obvious solution of contacting Hogwarts by owl, and he does not consider the consequences his actions might have for others. Once caught and punished, Harry is especially offended by the accusation that he wanted to call attention to himself. His fame means he always attracts interest, whether he wants it or not, and it pains him that people suspect that he enjoys and encourages the attention.

Getting Through Our Heads: One basic method authors employ to signal the importance of an idea is intentional repetition. In this chapter, Rowling repeats a single question three times: why couldn't Harry and Ron get through the barrier? Without the repetition, we might assume that the barrier always snaps shut a minute before the train leaves. But Rowling leaves no doubt that there is something suspicious about the boys' failure to get on the train.

CHAPTER SIX
Gilderoy Lockhart

At breakfast the next morning, Ron receives a Howler from Mrs. Weasley—a red envelope which, when opened, releases Mrs. Weasley's voice loudly lecturing Ron and telling him that Mr. Weasley is being investigated. Hermione thinks the boys deserved the Howler, but she makes friendly overtures to them, apparently satisfied that they have been sufficiently punished.

After breakfast, Harry, Ron, and Hermione head to the greenhouses for double Herbology class. **Professor Sprout**, the Herbology teacher, approaches with Gilderoy Lockhart. Sprout is bandaged and perturbed. Lockhart tells the students he has been showing her how to bandage a Whomping Willow and then pulls Harry aside. He says he probably gave Harry a "taste for publicity," but Harry should not fly an enchanted car just to get into the newspaper. Harry might have

DEADLY MANDRAKE

The mandrake, a real plant, is native to the Mediterranean region. It has forked roots and resembles the human form. Said to grow under gallows, the mandrake was often used by ancient people in curative and aphrodisiac potions. It contains a narcotic chemical. According to legend, uprooting a mandrake will cause it to scream, and anyone who hears the scream will die.

William Turner, c. 1652

earned fame from his first encounter with Voldemort, Lockhart says, but unlike Lockhart, Harry has not won "*Witch Weekly's* Most-Charming-Smile Award five times in a row."

Speechless, Harry returns to Herbology class, where Professor Sprout is showing the class how to repot Mandrakes. Mandrakes can undo curses, but their cries are fatal. The students put on earmuffs and watch as Sprout pulls up an ordinary-looking plant to reveal its roots: a screaming baby. She replants the Mandrake, and then the students practice on their own plants. Harry, Ron, and Hermione work with a Hufflepuff boy, **Justin Finch-Fletchley**, who chats animatedly.

After lunch, Harry meets a Gryffindor first year named **Colin Creevey** who wants to take Harry's picture and have him sign it. Draco Malfoy overhears Colin and teases Harry for handing out signed photos. Lockhart arrives and forces Harry to pose with him for a picture. Afterward, he warns Harry that handing out signed photos at his age looks egotistical.

In Defense Against the Dark Arts class, Lockhart gives a quiz consisting of fifty-four questions about himself. Hermione, who gets a perfect score, seems fascinated by Lockhart, but the other students quietly snicker at him. Lockhart releases a gaggle of Cornish pixies, which wreak havoc in the classroom. Lockhart hides under his desk. When the bell rings, he asks Harry, Ron, and Hermione to put the pixies back in their cage, and then leaves. Hermione defends Lockhart as they round up the pixies, but Ron says he doubts that Lockhart has done all the things he claims.

UNDERSTANDING AND INTERPRETING

Chapter Six

Patronizing and Incompetent: This chapter gives a clear look at the new Defense Against the Dark Arts teacher, Gilderoy Lockhart. In his interaction with his peers, such as Professor Sprout, Lockhart is bossy and patronizing, doling out self-satisfied advice in their fields of expertise. As a teacher in his own class, Lockhart proves himself unable to control the Dark Arts. The pixies destroy the classroom, hanging students from the ceiling and tossing wands out the window. Lockhart cannot stop them or recapture them. His incompetence makes us doubt that he is really an accomplished wizard, as he claims.

Struggles in the Spotlight: With a new group of Hogwarts first-years and the arrival of the publicity hound Gilderoy Lockhart, Harry must face the problems of fame. Lockhart misunderstands Harry's history, which he sees as a lucky break that Harry should use as a springboard to celebrity. But Harry wants to succeed on his merits, not on an accidental victory he can't remember. It humiliates him

J. K. Rowling

when people like Colin Creevey approach in awe. Special treatment makes him uncomfortable, especially since Draco Malfoy resentfully mocks Harry for getting attention. Lockhart identifies with Harry, giving him pointers on fame and involving him in photo sessions, which mortifies Harry. Lockhart will spare nothing in his quest of fame, while Harry longs only for normalcy.

CHAPTER SEVEN
Mudbloods and Murmurs

Early Saturday morning, **Oliver Wood**, captain of the Gryffindor Quidditch team, wakes Harry for practice. Colin Creevey follows Harry to the Quidditch field. Harry refuses to sign the picture of himself and Lockhart, but he does grudgingly explain the rules of Quidditch to Colin. In the dressing room, Wood talks at length about new strategies he has devised. Harry feels guilty that Gryffindor lost the Quidditch Cup last year. Harry missed the final match because he was in the hospital recovering from his encounter with Voldemort.

By the time the Quidditch players begin flying, Ron and Hermione have arrived. Colin takes pictures of the practice. The Slytherin Quidditch team arrives, and Wood tells **Marcus Flint**, the Slytherin captain, that Gryffindor has the field booked for the day. Flint hands Wood a note from Snape giving the Slytherins permission to train their new Seeker, Draco Malfoy. The Slytherins show off the expensive new brooms Malfoy's father bought for the whole team. Hermione and Ron arrive in the middle of the discussion, and Hermione accuses Malfoy of buying his way onto the team. Malfoy calls Hermione a "Mudblood," which causes a great uproar. Ron tries to cast a spell on Malfoy, but his broken wand backfires, causing him to burp up slugs, to the delight of the Slytherins.

Harry and Hermione take Ron to Hagrid's, where they wait for the spell to wear off. Lockhart has just left. Hagrid complains that Lockhart gave him useless advice and says that Lockhart got the teaching job because he was the only applicant. Hagrid and Ron explain to Hermione and Harry that "Mudblood" is an extremely derogatory word for someone with Muggle parent. Hagrid teases Harry about handing out signed photographs and shows off some huge pumpkins he is growing for Halloween.

That night Harry and Ron serve their detentions. Ron polishes silver with **Argus Filch**, the caretaker, while Harry addresses fan mail for Lockhart. Harry ignores Lockhart's endless monologue about fame until he hears a cold voice say, "Come to me. . . . Let me rip you. . . . Let me tear you. . . . Let me kill you." Lockhart says he cannot hear the voice. Harry tells Ron about the voice that night, and neither boy can think of a plausible explanation for it.

UNDERSTANDING AND INTERPRETING
Chapter Seven

Merit or Money: Rowling suggests that success can be achieved either with merit or with money. For Oliver Wood, succeeding on the Quidditch field involves spending his free time planning strategy and conducting long practices early in the morning. His work ethic is similar to Hermione's. She, like Wood, earns her high marks through hard work. The Slytherins, Malfoy in particular, do not see the point of hard work—not when victory can be easily bought. Malfoy's father bribed the team with fancy gifts so that Malfoy could play Seeker. The Slytherins expect their expensive brooms, not their strategy or skilled players, to help them triumph on the field. In contrast to Harry, who wants to earn the respect of his peers, Malfoy thinks he deserves automatic respect because he comes from an aristocratic family.

Muggles: Every time Malfoy comes on the scene, we see the bigotry that plagues the wizard world. Malfoy picks on Ron for his poverty, Hermione for her family, and Harry for his fame. However, Malfoy secretly envies them. In Chapter Four, he complains to his father that Hermione gets better grades than he does and that famous Harry gets to play Quidditch. Good grades, fame, and success at Quidditch require competency, talent, and hard work. Malfoy lacks all three, and he knows it. His jibes and taunts mask his deep insecurity. Malfoy's prejudice against "Mudbloods" is so vicious partly because his aristocratic lineage is one of the only things he truly does have. Malfoy clings desperately to his family name, demeaning the less exalted to make his own position more secure.

CHAPTER EIGHT
The Deathday Party

After Quidditch practice, Harry meets **Nearly Headless Nick**, the Gryffindor ghost, in a corridor. Nick has just received a letter turning down his request to join the Headless Hunt because his head is not completely separated from his body. **Mrs. Norris**, Filch's cat, arrives and stares at Harry. Filch comes along and takes Harry to his office to punish him for tracking mud into the building.

Filch is about to chastise Harry when a crashing noise sends him out of his office in pursuit of **Peeves**, the Hogwarts poltergeist. Harry reads a piece of mail on Filch's desk advertising Kwikspell, a correspondence course in magic. He wonders if Filch is a true wizard. When Filch returns, Harry denies reading the mail, but Filch seems flustered and sends Harry away. Harry meets Nick again and discovers that Nick told Peeves to distract Filch. Nick invites Harry to his deathday party on Halloween, and Harry reluctantly agrees to go.

Harry, Ron, and Hermione attend the deathday party in the dungeons instead of going to the feast in the Great Hall. The food is spoiled and rotting, and ghosts fill the air. Hermione tries to avoid **Moaning Myrtle**, a young ghost who haunts a toilet in a girls' bathroom, but Peeves makes sure Myrtle meets the children. Myrtle believes Hermione is making fun of her and leaves, crying. The members of the Headless Hunt arrive and upstage Nick's speech.

The children leave the party, and again Harry hears the sinister voice talking about killing. Ron and Hermione cannot hear it, but they follow Harry up to the second floor as he tries to follow the voice. He is convinced that whatever is speaking is going to kill someone. In a corridor they see a message written on the wall in large letters: "THE CHAMBER OF SECRETS HAS BEEN OPENED. ENE-MIES OF THE HEIR, BEWARE." There is a puddle of water on the floor, and Mrs. Norris, the cat, is hanging from a torch bracket. She is stiff and motionless, and her eyes are open. The rest of the students arrive and fall silent at the sight of Mrs. Norris and the message. Draco Malfoy says that the Mudbloods will be next.

UNDERSTANDING AND INTERPRETING
Chapter Eight

A Small Lesson: Chapter Eight illustrates the value of small kindnesses. Harry would much rather attend the Halloween feast than Nick's deathday party, but he sees how much his presence would mean to Nick and consents to go. This small act brings great joy to Nick. Hermione, on the other hand, carelessly hurts Moaning Myrtle's feelings. Her behavior illustrates the inverse of Harry's. If small kindnesses can bring great joy, small cruelties can cause great suffering.

Life After Death: Rowling's vision of wizard afterlife is an amusing, sad one. Not only do wizards experience life after death, their lives after death are nearly indistinguishable from normal existence. They enjoy different food and look slightly scary, but their personalities and experiences are unchanged. Peeves still acts bitter, mischievous, and vengeful. Nick still suffers at the hands of snobbish cliques. Myrtle is still self-conscious and miserable. None of these ghosts are particularly happy, but they get along. Rather terrifyingly, Rowling imagines an afterlife in which the only change is in the duration of existence.

CHAPTER NINE
The Writing on the Wall

Filch arrives and accuses Harry of killing Mrs. Norris. Dumbledore takes Harry, Ron, and Hermione to Lockhart's office. Dumbledore, McGonagall, and Snape examine the cat while Lockhart offers suggestions. Dumbledore pronounces Mrs. Norris not dead, but Petrified. Once the Mandrakes are mature, a potion can be made to restore her. Dumbledore says no second-year student could have Petrified the cat. Filch insists that Harry did it and says Harry knows Filch is a Squib. Snape presses the children to explain why they were in the corridor. Harry does not want to mention the voice. Snape says Harry is not telling the whole story and should be removed from the Quidditch team as punishment. Dumbledore says that Harry is innocent until proven guilty, and lets the children go.

Ron explains to Harry that a Squib is someone who has no magic powers, although he comes from wizard parents. At Hermione's instigation, **Professor Binns** explains the legend of the Chamber of Secrets in History of Magic class. **Salazar Slytherin**, one of the four founders of Hogwarts, believed that only pure-blooded wizards should attend the school. **Godric Gryffindor** disagreed, arguing with Slytherin about it. Slytherin left Hogwarts. According to the legend, Slytherin built a secret chamber in the castle containing a monster that would rid the school of all who were not pure-blooded. Only Slytherin's heir would be able to open the Chamber and control the monster.

Harry notices Justin Finch-Fletchley avoiding him and concludes that some students think he is Slytherin's heir. Harry, Ron, and Hermione inspect the area where Mrs. Norris was Petrified. They find scorch marks and a trail of spiders scurrying to escape the building. Ron admits he is afraid of spiders. They visit Moaning Myrtle, who lives in the bathroom next to the spot, but she says she did not see anything that night. Percy sees Ron emerging from a girls' toilet and angrily takes five points from Gryffindor.

Ron suggests Malfoy might be Slytherin's heir. Hermione says they should use a Polyjuice Potion to temporarily transform themselves into Slytherins. Disguised as Slytherins, they can interrogate Malfoy. A book in the Restricted Section of the library contains the recipe for the potion, so they will have to get a note from an unsuspecting teacher giving them permission to look at it.

Chapter Nine

Hermione Takes a Stand: Of the leading characters in the novel, Hermione is most threatened by Malfoy's diatribes against Muggles. To protect herself, she tries to learn as much as she can about the Chamber of Secrets and the Heir of Slytherin. She spends even more time than usual reading, attempting to ferret out information about the Chamber. She prods Professor Binns into recounting the legend of the Chamber. Finally, she suggests taking the Polyjuice Potion to find out if Malfoy is Slytherin's heir. She admits her plan involves breaking "about fifty school rules." Until this point, Hermione has been the one most likely to follow rules and to scold Harry and Ron for their disobedience. Her newly active role can be interpreted as self-interested, since by investigating she hopes to save herself. It can also be interpreted as selfless, since Hermione's investigative work might stem the rising tide of anti-Muggle sentiment and help all Muggles and half-Muggles at Hogwarts.

Worried Wizard: Worries plague Harry. The mysterious voice scares him, especially since no one else can hear it. Even Ron and Hermione, who usually understand Harry perfectly, cannot help him make sense of the voice. Harry frets over his mental health, as most teenagers do at some point, wondering what it means that he hears murderous voices in his head. Furthermore, Harry is worried that he could be a Slytherin. Evil, he thinks, might have the power to coax him to the Dark side against his wishes. In the first novel, Harry had to face his unwanted affinity with the Slytherins. The Sorting Hat pointed out that if Harry chose Slytherin, he could achieve fame and power. Although Harry does not like to think about it, some buried connection exists between himself and the Slytherins. Rowling emphasizes this latent connection by pointing out that some students consider Harry to be Slytherin's .

CHAPTER TEN
The Rogue Bludger

Lockhart's classes now consist of dramatizations of his supposed deeds. He frequently enlists Harry to help him perform these dramas. After class, Hermione flatters Lockhart and then convinces him to sign a slip allowing her to check out the book describing the Polyjuice Potion. The children hide in Moaning Myrtle's bathroom to read the recipe. Harry points out that some of the ingredients are only available in Snape's private stores. Hermione says she does not want to break the rules, but "threatening Muggle-borns is far worse than brewing up a difficult potion." Harry and Ron agree to help her.

Gryffindor plays Slytherin in a Quidditch match on a rainy morning. One of the Bludgers constantly chases Harry. Fred and George Weasley fly near Harry to protect him, blocking his view of the match. Gryffindor calls a time-out, and Harry convinces Wood to call off Fred and George and let him face the Bludger on his own. Harry spots the Snitch by Malfoy's head. Malfoy does not notice the Snitch because he is busy taunting Harry. The Bludger hits Harry, breaking his arm. Harry dives towards Malfoy, catching the Snitch with his good hand and holding on to the broom with his feet. Gryffindor wins.

Lockhart tries to tend to Harry, but his spell removes all the bones in Harry's arm. In the hospital wing, Madam Pomfrey sniffs at Lockhart's incompetence. She makes Harry drink a burning potion called Skele-Gro and warns him that regenerating bones is painful. Ron wonders how Hermione can still defend Lockhart.

Dobby visits Harry. He admits it was he who closed the barrier and kept Harry off the Hogwarts Express. He also admits to enchanting the Bludger in an attempt to injure Harry so badly he would have to go home. Harry is furious. Dobby explains that Harry has been a hero to his people, and he wants to protect Harry from the Chamber of Secrets, which is now open again. Dobby will not say who opened the Chamber before, nor why its opening threatens Harry, who is not Muggle-born. Dobby disappears when he hears footsteps.

Dumbledore and McGonagall enter, carrying a stiff body. There has been an attack on Colin Creevey, who was Petrified while holding his camera to his face. Dumbledore says "the Chamber of Secrets is indeed open again." He tells McGonagall that they should be asking not who opened the Chamber, but how it was opened.

Chapter Ten

Lovesick for Lockhart: Hermione is mature and exceptionally intelligent, qualities that do not preclude irrational lovesickness. Ron does not understand why Hermione cannot see through Lockhart's weak façade. It seems illogical that Hermione, an accomplished student, could suffer Lockhart's foolishness. But Hermione has a hard time discarding her old image of Lockhart and accepting the limitations of the man she now knows personally. Before returning to Hogwarts, Hermione conjured a picture of Lockhart, dreaming of the charming

HARRY POTTER AND LEOPARD
WALK UP TO DRAGON

In July 2002, the *Times* of London reported that a fake volume five of the Potter series was being sold in China. According to the *Times*, the book was titled *Harry Potter and Leopard Walk Up to Dragon*. In it, "Potter is transformed into a fat, hairy dwarf and stripped of his magic powers as he battles the forces of evil in the shape of a dragon."

smile rewarded by *Witch Weekly*, the sexy good looks featured on the covers of his books, and the manly heroism described by Lockhart himself. Understandably, she would rather believe in this imaginary he-man than recognize that her idol is actually an incompetent, vain buffoon.

It's Only a Game: The Gryffindor-Slytherin Quidditch match works as a metaphor for the conflict of good and evil that dominates the series. In both the game and the series, Harry is threatened. When his friends try to defend him from that threat, however, he cannot triumph. Only when he faces the threat alone can he prevail.

The match also emphasizes the hard work of the good guys and the cheating laziness of the bad guys. The Slytherins can afford the best broomsticks, but the Gryffindors have trained longer and harder than their opponents have. Malfoy, whose father bought him his place on the team, does not even notice the Snitch dangling inches from his face. Harry, in contrast, ignores Malfoy's jeers and heads determinedly toward the Snitch.

CHAPTER ELEVEN
The Dueling Club

Harry's bones grow back. He finds Ron and Hermione in Moaning Myrtle's bathroom, working on the Polyjuice Potion. He reports the news from Dobby, and they conclude that if the Chamber of Secrets has indeed been opened, Lucius Malfoy is the likely culprit.

Hermione says she will steal the final ingredients necessary for the potion if the others create a diversion. That Thursday, during Potions class, Harry tosses a firework into **Goyle**'s cauldron of Swelling Solution, causing it to explode. While Snape treats the students who have swollen body parts, Hermione sneaks into his office and steals the ingredients.

The students attend the first meeting of a Dueling Club only to discover that Lockhart, assisted by Snape, will be the instructor. In a demonstration of wizard dueling, Snape's spell hurls Lockhart against the wall. The students pair off, and Snape puts Harry and Malfoy together. Malfoy's first spell feels like a blow to the head, but Harry retaliates and hits Malfoy with a tickling spell. Malfoy hits Harry with a dancing spell. When Lockhart wants to use two students to demonstrate blocking spells, Snape suggests Harry and Malfoy.

Lockhart bumbles around as he tries to show Harry how to block a spell. Meanwhile, Snape whispers to Malfoy. Malfoy conjures a large snake that comes toward Harry. Lockhart tries to stop the snake, but he only enrages it and sends it toward Justin Finch-Fletchley. Harry tells the snake to stop, and it does. Justin storms from the room, and Hermione and Ron leave with Harry amid murmurs. They tell Harry he is a Parselmouth, one who speaks the language of snakes, and that Salazar Slytherin was famous for talking to snakes. Harry had not realized he was speaking Parseltongue. He understands now why he could communicate with the snake at the zoo.

Harry overhears some Hufflepuffs talking about him in the library, saying he must be Slytherin's heir. They believe Harry tried to make the snake attack Justin, who made the mistake of telling Harry he has Muggle parents. They say only Dark wizards are Parselmouths, and only a Dark wizard could have survived an attack by Voldemort. Harry interrupts and says he does not want to kill Muggle-borns.

In the hall he meets Hagrid, who complains of attacks on his roosters. Harry leaves Hagrid and continues along the corridors. He stumbles upon the Petrified body of Justin Finch-Fletchley and the Petrified ghost of Nearly Headless Nick. A trail of spiders is leaving the area. Peeves sees Harry and screams the news of the attack. McGonagall arrives and dispels the confusion. She takes Harry to a hidden spiral staircase, which moves like an escalator. Harry assumes they are going to see Dumbledore.

UNDERSTANDING AND INTERPRETING
Chapter Eleven

Self-Doubt and Solitude: Harry's realization that he is a Parselmouth makes him further doubt his identity. Much of the school is convinced that Harry is the Heir of Slytherin, and Muggle-born students fear for their lives in his presence. Harry knows he does not want to kill Muggle-born students, but he does not know if he is the Heir of Slytherin. He speaks Parseltongue, as Dark wizards do, and the Sorting Hat first suggested Slytherin, home of Dark wizards, before agreeing to place him in Gryffindor. It is plausible that Harry has been unconsciously fighting to stave off the darkness that exists in him. In the first novel in the series, Harry struggled to overcome the stigma of his unearned fame; in the second novel, he must struggle to overcome the stigma of unearned infamy.

Snape the Snake? Professor Snape seems intent on encouraging animosity between Harry and Malfoy, but his true feelings about Harry are ambiguous. Perhaps he told Malfoy to conjure the snake so that Harry would speak to it and rouse the suspicions of his peers. Perhaps he has genuine suspicions that Harry is Slytherin's heir. Perhaps he agrees with Malfoy that Muggle-borns have no place at Hogwarts, or perhaps he thinks they do. Snape is one of the most enigmatic figures in the novel. One of the only things we know for certain about Snape is that he dislikes Harry Potter.

CHAPTER TWELVE
The Polyjuice Potion

Left alone in Dumbledore's office, Harry puts on the Sorting Hat, wanting to make sure it put him in the right house. The hat tells him he would have done well in Slytherin, and Harry yanks it off. A "decrepit-looking" bird bursts into flames as Harry watches. Dumbledore arrives and explains that the bird is his pet phoenix, Fawkes. A baby bird emerges from the ashes. Dumbledore says phoenixes can carry heavy loads and their tears have healing powers.

Hagrid rushes in, defending Harry and saying he did not attack Justin. Dumbledore says he knows Harry did not attack Justin and asks Harry if there is anything he wants to tell him. Harry thinks hard about all his secrets but says nothing.

On Christmas morning, Hermione announces that the Polyjuice Potion is ready. After the feast, Harry and Ron leave two chocolate cakes filled with a sleeping potion where **Crabbe** and Goyle will find them. The Slytherins eat the cakes and fall

"C. S. Lewis, author of brilliant Christian apologetics, had a not-at-all-hidden agenda in the Narnia chronicles: He was asserting that a longing for the supernatural is natural. Rowling's aim, aside from robust fun, seems to be to show the complexity of children, and the ambiguities of childhood—the delights and fears of separation and exploration."

GEORGE WILL

unconscious. Harry and Ron take a few of their hairs and then lock the Slytherins in a closet. With the hairs, they can complete the potion. Hermione uses a hair she got from **Milicent Bulstrode**'s robe at the Dueling Club. After drinking the potion, Harry and Ron transform into Crabbe and Goyle. Hermione refuses to emerge from her stall, and Harry and Ron must leave without her.

They find Malfoy, who takes them to the Slytherin common room. He shows them a newspaper clipping that says Mr. Weasley has been fined fifty Galleons for the enchanted car. Lucius Malfoy is calling for his resignation. Malfoy insults the Weasleys and derides Dumbledore for loving Muggle-borns. He says he wishes he knew the identity of Slytherin's heir. His father will not tell him about the first time the Chamber of Secrets was opened, but he knows it happened fifty years ago. He tells them a Mudblood died in the melee, and the person who opened the Chamber was expelled. Malfoy thinks the perpetrator is in Azkaban, the wizard prison. Lucius Malfoy's house was raided recently, but all the Dark Arts material is safely hidden in a secret vault under the drawing-room floor.

Harry and Ron start to turn back into themselves and must rush to Moaning Myrtle's bathroom. They find Hermione still hidden in her stall. She accidentally used a hair of Milicent Bulstrode's cat, and the potion gave her a furry face, pointed ears, and a tail.

UNDERSTANDING AND INTERPRETING
Chapter Twelve

Trusting Dumbledore: Harry does not know what to expect in Dumbledore's office, and what he faces surprises him: a kind invitation to share anything that might be troubling him. Dumbledore does not want Harry to admit to wrongdoing; he wants him to confess his troubles and relieve his mind. Dumbledore does not press Harry for information. Instead, he treats Harry respectfully, giving him an opportunity to unburden himself, but trusting that if Harry does not want to speak, he has good reasons for his silence. When Dumbledore asks, "Is there . . . anything you'd like to tell me?" he is really asking, "are you safe? Can you handle the danger on your own?"

While Ron and Harry fail to find the Heir of Slytherin, they do learn of the secret vault under the Malfoy Manor. They also hear still more evidence of the Slytherins' snobbery and witness the stupidity of Slytherin house residents. Crabbe and Goyle idiotically eat the cake Hermione left near the staircase without wondering why it happens to be sitting there. That Ron and Harry, who are clueless, successfully pass themselves off as Slytherins, suggests that cluelessness is Crabbe's and Goyle's natural state. Ron notes that when Harry looks bewildered, he resembles Goyle precisely. The password to the Slytherin common room is "pure blood," an indication of the house's preoccupation. The Slytherins' single-minded bigotry contrasts with the Gryffindors' eclecticism, which is typified by their ever-changing password.

CHAPTER THIRTEEN
The Very Secret Diary

Hermione stays in the hospital wing for several weeks, recovering from the ill effects of the potion. Outside Moaning Myrtle's bathroom, the boys hear a commotion and discover more water in the hall. Myrtle tells them, sobbing, that someone threw a book into her toilet. Ron warns Harry against looking at the soggy volume, saying it could be enchanted, but Harry picks it up anyway. It is the blank diary of **T. M. Riddle**. Ron remembers polishing school trophies once and seeing the name T. M. Riddle. Fifty years ago, Riddle won a Special Award for Services to the School.

When Hermione returns from the hospital, she suggests Riddle received his commendation for "catching the Heir of Slytherin." She tries and fails to make writing appear in the diary. In the trophy room, Harry discovers that Riddle was Head Boy.

Lockhart takes credit for stopping the attacks. As a "morale-booster," he decorates the Great Hall for Valentine's Day and sends dwarves around the school delivering valentines. Harry is accosted by a dwarf with a singing valentine. When he tries to escape, his bag rips and ink spills all over his books. Malfoy picks up Riddle's diary in the confusion, but Harry gets it back with a disarming charm. Percy scolds him for doing magic in the hall.

> "The plots reinforce the theme that evil is real, and must be courageously opposed. As this theme unfolds, so do the characters of Harry and his friends. They develop courage, loyalty, and a willingness to sacrifice for one another — even at the risk of their lives. Not bad lessons in a self-centered world."
>
> **CHUCK COLSON**, "WITCHES AND WIZARDS: THE HARRY POTTER PHENOMENON"

Harry sees that none of the ink he spilled stained the diary. He tries to write a message in the book, and his words dissolve into a reply from Tom Riddle. Harry asks Tom about the Chamber of Secrets. Tom says he caught the person who opened the Chamber, but the Headmaster, **Professor Dippet**, covered up the incident, and the perpetrator was not imprisoned. A diary entry dissolves into a screen. Harry looks down at the screen and finds himself falling through it into the Headmaster's office, where Riddle is complaining of the Muggle orphanage he must live in over the summer. Dippet says that as a half-blood with a

Muggle father, he will be safer away from Hogwarts. Riddle implies that he will catch the person who opened the Chamber. In the dungeons, Riddle confronts another student, a large boy who denies that the creature he is hiding has killed anybody. Riddle tries to stop both the boy and the creature with a spell, but the creature, a huge spider, gets away. Harry finds himself back in bed. He tells Ron what he saw, saying, "Hagrid opened the Chamber of Secrets."

UNDERSTANDING AND INTERPRETING
Chapter Thirteen

Mysterious Diary: Something about Riddle's diary attracts and fascinates Harry. He begins acting strange, ignoring Ron's warning and looking at the diary for hours, even though it is full of blank pages. Harry returns to the diary again and again, usually in private. The secrecy with which Harry examines the diary puts us on edge. Harry seems to have an intuitive sense of the diary's danger, or a fear that by looking at it he is doing something wrong.

A Spotty Picture: Riddle shows Harry enough of the past to make him believe that Hagrid was responsible for the first round of attacks. A more skeptical viewer than Harry, however, would notice a number of blank spots in the picture Riddle paints. Harry does not see the Chamber, and he does not see Hagrid's monstrous creature attack anyone. He does not see a reasonable explanation for Hagrid's defensive behavior. He sees only what Riddle wants him to see, and concludes from the evidence presented that Riddle was a decent, conscientious boy, much like Harry himself, who did everything he could to save Hogwarts.

CHAPTER FOURTEEN
Cornelius Fudge

Harry, Ron, and Hermione discuss Hagrid and the monstrous spider Harry saw. They cannot believe Hagrid would hurt anyone on purpose, but they can easily imagine him rescuing a creature trapped in a secret chamber. They decide not to broach the subject with Hagrid unless another attack occurs. The second-years choose their subjects for next year. Hermione signs up for everything, and Harry picks the same courses as Ron.

On the eve of the next Quidditch match, Harry finds his room ransacked and Riddle's diary gone. He, Ron, and Hermione conclude that a Gryffindor must be to blame, since the other students do not know the Gryffindor password. On the morning of the match, Harry hears the disembodied voice again. Hermione announces she has "just understood something" and runs off to the library. The match is just about to begin when McGonagall arrives and cancels it, telling everyone to return to his or her common room. She takes Harry and Ron to the hospital wing, where they see that Hermione has been Petrified. Penelope Clearwater, a Ravenclaw prefect, has also been Petrified.

Severe restrictions are placed on all of the students. Harry and Ron use the invisibility cloak to sneak out to Hagrid's. Before they can ask him anything, they must hide under the cloak again, as Dumbledore and **Cornelius Fudge**, the Minister of Magic, arrive. Fudge says he must take Hagrid away in order to appear productive. Dumbledore insists that Hagrid's removal will not help. Lucius Malfoy arrives with a letter signed by the twelve governors of Hogwarts calling for Dumbledore's suspension. Fudge objects to this, but Malfoy is adamant. Before the men leave the cabin, Dumbledore looks to where Harry is hiding and says he will "only *truly* have left this school when none here are loyal to me," adding that those at Hogwarts who ask for help will always receive it. As Hagrid leaves, he says that anyone wanting to "find out some *stuff*" should follow the spiders. He also mentions loudly that someone will have to feed his dog, **Fang**, while he is gone.

Chapter Fourteen

Harry and Ron: By the end of Chapter Fourteen, Ron and Harry have been robbed of their usual allies and burdened with great responsibility. Hermione, who seemed on the verge of solving the mystery through research and persistence, has been Petrified. Hagrid, a loyal if bumbling friend, is on his way to Azkaban, the wizard prison. Dumbledore, the source of all good power at Hogwarts and the only wizard of whom Voldemort was afraid, has been unceremoniously dismissed. Mr. Malfoy, sinister and obnoxious as ever, has more power than ever before, as represented by his astonishing authority to banish Dumbledore. The fact that Hagrid and Dumbledore give last-minute instructions to Harry and Ron suggests that the men place their trust in the students, which puts a burden on the boys. Harry and Ron must try to save their school without Hermione's brains, Hagrid's friendship, or Dumbledore's wisdom.

Fudging the Job: In Cornelius Fudge, Rowling gives us a model of governmental inadequacy. As Minister of Magic, Fudge holds an important post—one for which he seems severely under-qualified. In the first novel in the series, the sole mention of Fudge comes from Hagrid, who calls him a "bungler." Here, Rowling describes Fudge's "anxious expression" and "uncomfortabl[e]" conversation. He fidgets, complains of the pressure he is under, and refuses to look Hagrid in the eye. He freely admits that he wants to jail Hagrid not because it will solve any-thing, but because it will make him look like he is taking important action. Fudge's name fits him perfectly since he would rather "fudge" and make some-thing up than actually do the job correctly. In comparison with Fudge, Malfoy is a paragon of powerful leadership. The public interest may not motivate him, but at least he carries out his plans swiftly, efficiently, and ruthlessly. Whereas Fudge bows to pressure from others, Malfoy pressures others, managing to obtain the signatures of the governors.

CHAPTER FIFTEEN
Aragog

Harry and Ron cannot visit Hermione, since the new regulations forbid visits to the hospital wing. Harry puzzles over Dumbledore's parting words. Further-more, he and Ron have not seen any spiders to follow, as Hagrid suggested. Of the students, only Malfoy seems happy, bragging that his father got rid of Dumbledore and encouraging Snape to apply for the job of Headmaster. **Ernie Macmillan**, the Hufflepuff who suspected Harry of opening the Chamber, apol-ogizes, saying he knows that Harry would not harm Hermione.

Harry and Ron see spiders crawling toward the Forbidden Forest. That night, they use the invisibility cloak to sneak out. They retrieve Fang from Hagrid's cot-tage and follow the spiders. To their surprise, Mr. Weasley's car is wandering in the forest. Harry, Ron, and Fang are captured by three giant spiders and carried to a hollow filled with other spiders as big as horses.

An old blind spider named **Aragog** orders them to be executed. Harry says that they are friends of Hagrid and tells him Hagrid is in trouble because of attacks on the students. Aragog explains that Hagrid was originally expelled from Hogwarts because people thought he, Aragog, was the monster from the Cham-ber of Secrets, which he is not. Hagrid raised Aragog from an egg and has always cared for him. Aragog will only tell Harry that the spiders never name the crea-ture that lives in the Chamber. This unnamed creature killed a girl in a bathroom.

Even though Harry and Ron know Hagrid, Aragog will not spare them. As the other spiders close in on them, Mr. Weasley's enchanted car comes roaring through the hollow. The boys jump in with Fang and escape. The car leaves them at the edge of the forest. Ron, scared even of tiny spiders, is furious with Hagrid. Back in the dormitory, Ron falls asleep, but Harry lies awake thinking about what he has learned. Hagrid did not open the Chamber, as Riddle implied. Harry realizes something and wakes up Ron. He explains that the girl killed in the bathroom might be Moaning Myrtle.

UNDERSTANDING AND INTERPRETING
Chapter Fifteen

Naming the Enemy: Naming one's enemies, Rowling suggests, is a key step in conquering them. Dumbledore and Harry always call Voldemort by his name instead of referring to him as He-Who-Must-Not-Be-Named, or You-Know-Who, as almost everyone else does. Calling him Voldemort defines him and dilutes his power. "Voldemort" is a manageable word like "Dumbledore" or "Harry," and using it puts the villain on a manageable level. Referring to him as He-Who-Must-Not-Be-Named makes him dangerous, uncontained, and unimaginable. However, Voldemort is imaginable; he is an ordinary, if highly talented, wizard who went astray. The community of spiders, including Aragog himself, refuses to name the creature in the Chamber. Because they do not dare to name their enemy, they live in the woods, hidden far away from the undefeated creature. In contrast, Harry and Dumbledore can face Voldemort with confidence, partly because they dare to name him.

Bighearted Hagrid: Hagrid is not a stupid man, but he lets his warm heart rule his head. He feels concern and sympathy for all creatures, even monsters. Ron sums up Hagrid's problem, saying, "He always thinks monsters aren't as bad as they're made out." Hagrid cannot think ill of any being he loves, whether that being is a giant spider or Harry. It was Hagrid's love of Aragog that led to his expulsion. His inability to think cynically probably sealed his fate, since he would never suspect Riddle of wrongdoing. Rowling suggests that, while we should be kind and optimistic, we should not let kindness and optimism overwhelm common sense and intelligence. If we do, we risk hurting ourselves and others.

CHAPTER SIXTEEN
The Chamber of Secrets

The students are surprised when McGonagall announces that exams will begin in one week. Harry feels unprepared. A few days later, at breakfast, McGonagall says the Mandrakes are mature, which means that the Petrified victims will be revived that night. Ginny Weasley sits next to Ron and Harry and says she wants to tell them something, but when Percy arrives, she runs off. Percy says she saw him "doing something," and he asked her not to tell anyone.

THE BASILISK ❧ The legend of the Basilisk has persisted since the days of ancient Rome. Medieval folklore describes the Basilisk as a snake with a rooster's head. Some Basilisks breathe fire, and others can kill with a glance. A Basilisk dies if it sees its own reflection. Its natural enemies are the weasel, and the rooster, at whose call it suffers instant death.

Harry and Ron talk Lockhart into letting the Gryffindors walk to class unescorted, and then the boys steal away to Moaning Myrtle's bathroom. McGonagall catches them, and they say they were going to see Hermione. McGonagall gives them permission to visit their friend. In Hermione's hand, they find a piece of paper describing the Basilisk, a giant snake that can kill by looking into its victim's eyes. Spiders run from the Basilisk. The rooster's crow kills it.

Harry and Ron realize that the creature in the Chamber is a Basilisk. Its Hogwarts victims are still alive only because they did not look directly at it. The Basilisk's presence explains the killing of Hagrid's roosters and the flight of the spiders. The voice Harry heard was the voice of the Basilisk. Only he could hear it because only he understands Parseltongue.

Hermione has written "pipes" on the paper, and the boys deduce that the creature has been moving about in the plumbing. They suspect the entrance to the Chamber is in Moaning Myrtle's bathroom. The boys are on their way to tell McGonagall of their discoveries when they hear an announcement ordering all students back to their dormitories. Hiding in the staff room, Ron and Harry hear that Ginny Weasley has been taken to the Chamber by the creature. When Lockhart arrives in the staff room, the other teachers tell him he can do battle with the creature, since he has been bragging about his abilities. He leaves looking frightened.

That night, Harry and Ron go to see Lockhart. They find him packing his bags. He tells them he did not really do the things described in his books. He stole the stories other people told him, putting a Memory Charm on the storytellers. Lockhart tries to put such a charm on the boys, but Harry uses a disarming curse, and Ron throws Lockhart's wand out the window.

They take Lockhart to Moaning Myrtle's bathroom. They ask her how she died, and she eagerly gives an account of staring into a pair of yellow eyes and then leaving her body. Harry sees a little snake drawn on the side of a pipe under the sink. He speaks Parseltongue to it, and the sink slides aside, revealing a huge open pipe. They slide down it, making Lockhart go first. In the passage at the bottom, they come across a giant snakeskin. Lockhart grabs Ron's wand and tries to erase the boys' memories, but the broken wand backfires and destroys his own memory. The wand also causes the roof of the tunnel to collapse, separating Harry from Ron and Lockhart. Harry continues on until he comes to a wall adorned with serpents. In Parseltongue, he commands the wall to open, and walks through the portal that appears.

UNDERSTANDING AND INTERPRETING
Chapter Sixteen

The Victim Solves the Mystery: Ron once said that Hermione solves everything by going to the library. Her technique works here. She solved the mystery through research, and even lying Petrified in a hospital bed, Hermione now helps Harry and Ron. Hermione's intellect and scholarship are her most important strengths, so it is fitting that her contribution is represented by a bit of research scribbled on a piece of paper.

A Hero Falls: Among the many mysteries cleared up in this chapter is the mystery of Lockhart. Under pressure from the other teachers to live up to his reputation, and faced with the prospect of fighting a monster, Lockhart's façade finally crumbles. He reacts to urgent danger by packing his bags and trying to run away. When the boys catch him and force him to go underground, he thinks only of his own safety and of preserving his unearned reputation. Ron and Harry look most impressive when compared to Lockhart. Although they know little about the Dark Arts and nothing about defeating a Basilisk, they go to the Chamber to find Ginny. Strength of character has nothing to do with age, position, reputation, or fame. When character is needed most, Harry and Ron rise to the occasion, while Lockhart crumbles.

CHAPTER SEVENTEEN
The Heir of Slytherin

Harry finds Ginny lying unconscious at the foot of a huge statue of a wizard. He sees a hazy image of Tom Riddle. Tom says he is a memory preserved in a diary. Tom's diary is lying on the floor. Harry asks Tom to help him move Ginny, but he refuses, and when Harry sets down his wand to go to Ginny, Tom takes it.

Tom explains that Ginny has been writing to him in his diary for many months. He has feigned compassion for her and gained power through the secrets she confided to him. He began to tell her his own secrets on order to control her. Under his influence, Ginny opened the Chamber and told the Basilisk to attack the half-Muggles. When Ginny stopped trusting the diary, she threw it in Moaning Myrtle's toilet, and Harry found it. Riddle admits that he, not Hagrid, was the one who opened the Chamber fifty years ago. Only Dumbledore believed in Hagrid's innocence.

Riddle says he is more interested in killing Harry than in killing Mudbloods. Ginny stole back the diary from Harry, worried that he would learn her secrets. Riddle forced Ginny to come to the Chamber, knowing Harry would follow. Tom uses Harry's wand to trace the letters of his name, "Tom Marvolo Riddle," in the air. He rearranges them to read "I am Lord Voldemort," and proclaims himself the greatest wizard in the world. Tom Riddle was his original name, but he hated it because it had come from his Muggle father, so he chose Voldemort. Harry tells Voldemort he is not the greatest wizard—Dumbledore holds that title.

Dumbledore's phoenix, Fawkes, flies into the Chamber, bringing Harry the Sorting Hat. Voldemort scoffs at these offerings from Dumbledore and demands to know how Harry defeated him when he was a baby. Harry says his mother died to save him. Riddle seems relieved, saying, "There is nothing special about you," and pointing out "strange likenesses" between himself and Harry.

Voldemort calls the Basilisk and tells it to kill Harry. When the huge Basilisk emerges, Fawkes pecks out its eyes. Fawkes drops the Sorting Hat on Harry, who puts it on and calls for help. A sword falls out of the hat and its hilt hits Harry. Harry clasps the sword and stabs the serpent through the roof of its mouth, but not before a poisonous fang breaks off in his arm. He pulls the fang out. Riddle tells Harry he will die, but Fawkes sheds tears into Harry's wound, healing it. Fawkes drops the

> "Can anyone wonder at the fabulous sales success of these books? The Harry Potter series is a supernatural version of *Tom Brown's School Days*, updated and given a hip this-is-how-kids-really-are shine. And Harry is the kid most children feel themselves to be, adrift in a world of unimaginative and often unpleasant adults—Muggles, Rowling calls them—who neither understand them nor care to. Harry is, in fact, a male Cinderella, waiting for someone to invite him to the ball."
>
> **STEPHEN KING**

diary in Harry's lap. Harry looks at it for a moment and then stabs it with the Basilisk fang. Riddle screams and disappears. Ginny wakes up, and the two return to Ron, who has dug a passage through the fallen stones. They also find Lockhart. Harry grasps Fawkes's tail feathers, and Ginny and Lockhart hold onto Ron, who clutches Harry's robe. Fawkes flies them all back up the pipe to Moaning Myrtle's bathroom and then leads them to McGonagall's office.

UNDERSTANDING AND INTERPRETING
Chapter Seventeen

Riddle's Crime: Ginny is the picture of innocence at the beginning of the novel, nursing her schoolgirl crush on Harry and looking up to her siblings. Voldemort robs her of that innocence. He takes her into his trust, and she shares intimate secrets with him. Voldemort betrays her trust by forcing her to commit crimes she never would have committed willingly, even inducing her to order murder. Harry worried about his possible affinity with Slytherin, but his worries can dissipate now that the mystery is explained. Ginny must worry for the rest of her life, wondering how she could have commanded the murder of Half-Muggles and Muggles, and worrying that Voldemort saw something particularly malleable in her character.

Confidence Rewarded: Dumbledore rewards the trust Harry placed in him. Before Dumbledore left Hogwarts, he said he would only have left the school for good when "none here are loyal to me," and that those who ask for help at Hogwarts will receive it. Harry expresses his loyalty to Dumbledore, calling him "the greatest wizard in the world," and immediately afterward Fawkes arrives with the Sorting Hat. Although Harry has often been hailed as a great wizard, and although he is the only person ever to have survived an attack by Voldemort, he does not claim greatness or power for himself. Instead, Harry praises Dumbledore and finds his loyalty rewarded.

CHAPTER EIGHTEEN
Dobby's Reward

In McGonagall's office, Mr. and Mrs. Weasley embrace Ginny. Dumbledore is also there. Harry explains how they found the entrance to the Chamber, and McGonagall remarks that they broke "a hundred school rules" in the process. Harry narrates his battle with the Basilisk but does not mention the diary, for fear of getting Ginny in trouble. Dumbledore wonders how Voldemort

ANCESTOR OR DESCENDENT?

Inevitably, a long series like the Harry Potter saga will contain a few inconsistencies and errors. Fans have delighted in combing the novels for problems, some of which have been fixed in subsequent printings. Among the most embarrassing must be the assertion, in this chapter, that Tom Riddle was an ancestor, rather than a descendent, of Salazar Slytherin.

enchanted Ginny. When Harry realizes Dumbledore will not blame Ginny, he explains the diary. Dumbledore says Ginny will not be punished.

Dumbledore sends McGonagall off to plan a feast while he talks with Harry and Ron. He says they will each receive Special Awards for Service to the School, and he awards four hundred points to Gryffindor. When Dumbledore tries to talk to Lockhart, Ron explains the backfiring Memory Charm. Ron takes Lockhart to the infirmary.

Dumbledore thanks Harry for his loyalty. Harry blurts out Voldemort's claim that Harry is like him. He confesses that the Sorting Hat said he would do well in Slytherin, and says he worries about his ability to speak Parseltongue. Dumbledore explains that Harry received the ability to speak Parseltongue the night Voldemort tried to kill him. Apparently, some of Voldemort's powers transferred to Harry. Dumbledore admits that Harry has qualities that Salazar Slytherin valued: "resourcefulness—determination—a certain disregard for rules."

The difference between Harry and Voldemort, he says, is that Harry asked to be placed in Gryffindor. "It is our choices, Harry," he says, "that

> "You may come from a bad family or a good family; but it's choices you make that make you WHO you are. I come from a good family, but I still have to make good choices to keep it going."
>
> **TAYLOR NEAL**, AGE ELEVEN, FROM AN ESSAY CONTEST ENTRY CALLED "TOP TEN THINGS I LEARNED FROM THE HARRY POTTER BOOKS"

show what we truly are, far more than our abilities." Dumbledore shows Harry that the sword he used to slay the Basilisk belonged to Godric Gryffindor.

Lucius Malfoy arrives, accompanied by Dobby. He asks Dumbledore how he dares return. Dumbledore explains that the other eleven school governors asked him to come back when Ginny disappeared. Some have claimed that Malfoy made them sign Dumbledore's Order of Suspension by threatening their families. Dumbledore sarcastically remarks it is lucky Ginny was cleared, since it would have harmed the Weasley family greatly—not to mention the Muggle Protection Act that Mr. Weasley supports—if someone had fingered her as a murderous pure-blood girl killing Muggle-borns of her own free will.

Dobby keeps pointing at Malfoy and then at Riddle's diary. Harry understands and accuses Mr. Malfoy of giving Riddle's diary to Ginny by slipping it into one of her books at Flourish and Blotts. Dumbledore admits that no one will able to prove Malfoy's guilt, but he warns him against handing out Voldemort relics to susceptible students in the future.

TOM BROWN'S SCHOOL DAYS

The first widely successful boarding school novel, *Tom Brown's School Days*, was written by Thomas Hughes and published in 1857. In the novel, Tom attends Rugby School under the famous headmaster Dr. Thomas Arnold. He describes Arnold in words Harry might use to describe Dumbledore, calling him

Thomas Hughes (1822–1896)

"a man whom we felt to be, with all his heart and soul and strength, striving against whatever was mean and unmanly and unrighteous in our little world."

Malfoy leaves, kicking Dobby. Harry takes off a dirty sock and shoves the diary into it. He chases after Mr. Malfoy and gives him the diary. Malfoy rips off the sock and tosses it away, but Dobby catches it. Malfoy has given Dobby an article of clothing, which means that Dobby is free. Malfoy is enraged at losing his slave, but Dobby protects Harry from Malfoy's wand and sends Lucius tumbling downstairs.

At the feast, Hermione and Hagrid return, Gryffindor wins the house cup, and exams are cancelled. Lucius Malfoy loses his position as a school governor. On the Hogwarts Express home, Ginny explains Percy's odd behavior, revealing that he has a girlfriend, Penelope Clearwater. She saw them kissing. Harry gives his phone number to Ron and Hermione.

UNDERSTANDING AND INTERPRETING
Chapter Eighteen

Family Feud: Though readers think of Draco Malfoy as Harry's nemesis, it becomes clear in this chapter that the Malfoys, at least as a family, worry more about the Weasleys than they do about Harry. Many skirmishes underline this feud. Early in the novel, Lucius Malfoy and Arthur Weasley came to blows. Harry and Draco constantly squabble. Lucius Malfoy attempted to set up Ginny Weasley for expulsion from Hogwarts. If he had succeeded, Mr. Weasley certainly would have fallen into disrepute. The prominent Malfoys go to such great lengths to discredit the Weasleys, because they are an upstanding, pure-blood wizarding family who support Muggles and half-Muggles wholeheartedly. To discredit the Weasleys is to cast doubt on all Muggle-supporting wizards. The Muggle Protection Act, which Mr. Weasley backs, particularly provokes the ire of Mr. Malfoy.

Uncomfortable Explanations: Harry still worries about his similarities to Slytherins, and Dumbledore does not deny that the similarities exist. He admits that Harry possesses many of the attributes most highly prized by Slytherin and his descendent, Voldemort. However, Dumbledore says, by the exercise of free will, Harry can use his skills for good, not evil. Rowling's implication is that great people, whether they are great in the realm of good or evil, come from the same basic material. Harry is not naturally moral, and Voldemort is not naturally immoral. They are both naturally intelligent, quick, and skilled. What they do with their basic makeup is up to them. Dumbledore's explanation is not an especially comfortable one. He does not soothe Harry and tell him that he has nothing in common with Slytherins. Rather, he suggests Harry has the capacity for evil and must exercise vigilance and actively choose not to misuse his powers.

Conclusions

Gilderoy Lockhart stands out as an especially colorful edition to the Potter universe. Of *Harry Potter and the Chamber of Secrets*, Lee Siegel has written, "I cannot think of any 'adult' fiction that attempts genuinely to satirize the celebrity-fraud." With Lockhart, Rowling satirizes a contemporary archetype rather than a more traditional one. It is easy to imagine Lockhart gracing the pages of *People* magazine and saturating popular culture. Like many modern celebrities, Lockhart is famous mostly for being famous. His "work" is completely fraudulent and he possesses neither courage nor talent.

Following the publication of the Harry Potter series in America, a great deal of publicity surrounded the small number of conservative Christians who protested the novels, claiming that they promote witchcraft and the occult. Despite the objections of some Christians, who thought the Potter books flouted a biblical injunction against witchcraft and replaced the authority of God with magic, most Christians have not only defended the books, but have even pointed to Christian lessons in Harry's story. Commentator Chuck Colson has noted that the magic in the books is "mechanical" and not the kind of "occultic" magic that attempts to draw on supernatural powers of evil. In the book *What's a Christian to Do with Harry Potter?*, Connie Neal interprets the novels through a Christian lens. She focuses on Dumbledore's explanation of why the Sorting Hat put Harry in Gryffindor: "It is our choices, Harry, that show what we truly are, far more than our abilities."

> "Once again, the attraction of Rowling's traditional British school story is magnified tenfold by the fantasy elements superimposed upon it. The atmosphere Rowling creates is unique; the story whizzes along; Harry is an unassuming and completely sympathetic hero. But, truth to tell, you may feel as if you've read it all before. Rowling clearly hit on a winning formula with the first Harry Potter book; the second book—though still great fun—feels a tad, well, formulaic."
>
> **THE HORN BOOK MAGAZINE**

IV

HARRY POTTER AND THE PRISONER OF AZKABAN

Key Facts

Genre: Children's novel, boarding-school novel, bildungsroman; the third in a planned series of seven novels

Date of First Publication: 1999

Setting: An unspecified, roughly modern time in England; London, Hogwarts School of Witchcraft and Wizardry, and the wizarding village of Hogsmeade

Narrator: Anonymous, third-person observer

Plot Overview: Hogwarts is being guarded by dementors searching for an escaped wizard-murderer named Sirius Black. Using a Marauder's Map given to him by the Weasley twins, Harry sneaks into Hogsmeade and overhears a conversation about how Sirius Black betrayed Lily and James Potter to Voldemort. One night, a black dog attacks Ron and drags him under the Whomping Willow and through a passage to the Shrieking Shack in Hogsmeade. Harry and Hermione follow and discover Sirius Black, an Animagus who can become a dog. We learn that Sirius was not the one who betrayed the Potters. The children help Sirius escape.

Style, Technique, and Language

Style and Technique—In a Name: Almost all of the names in the Harry Potter series are significant. Sirius Black means "Black Dog." The name Remus Lupin has its origins in the Latin word for wolf and in the name of one of Rome's founders, Remus, who was suckled by a wolf. Lucius Malfoy's name perfectly sums up his personality. In many languages, "mal" means "bad," and "Lucius" is similar to "Lucifer." Other names, like Dumbledore, have actual definitions—in this case, "bumblebee" in Old English. Professor Trelawney's first name is Sibyll; Sibyll was the ancient prophet of mythology. Furthermore, Padfoot, Moony, Wormtail, and Prongs are names that conjure up the animals they represent.

Language—Simplistic, Engaging: Surprising everyone from the author to the publishers to critics, Harry Potter has found tremendous popularity among adults.

Some critics have derided this popularity as indicative of the public's underwhelming reading habits, while others have praised Rowling for bridging the generation gap and writing books parents can enjoy with their children. Simplistic prose aside, adults enjoy the novels for the same reasons children do—they are well-crafted narratives with memorable characters that address universal issues. Some readers, however, wonder why Rowling's novels appeal to adults who might be expected to get more enjoyment from the works of fantasy writers E. Nesbit and Edward Eager.

Characters in *Harry Potter and the Prisoner of Azkaban*

Hannah Abbott: A Hufflepuff student.

Katie Bell: A Chaser for the Gryffindor Quidditch team.

Professor Binns: A ghost who teaches History of Magic.

Sirius Black: An accused murderer who has escaped from Azkaban. He is an Animagus and can turn into a dog. Initially, Harry thinks Sirius Black betrayed his parents, Lily and James Potter. He is Harry's godfather.

Boggart: A shape-shifting spirit that shies away from laughter. A boggart takes the shape of whatever the viewer most fears—in Harry's case, a dementor.

Bole: A Beater for the Slytherin Quidditch team.

Lavender Brown: A student at Hogwarts. Lavender loves Professor Trelawney and believes all of the professor's predictions. A fox kills Lavender's pet rabbit.

Buckbeak: A hippogriff that attacks Malfoy on the first day of class after Malfoy ignores Hagrid's injunction against insulting the creatures. Buckbeak is condemned to death but escapes with the help of Harry and Hermione.

Sir Cadogan: A clumsy, cartoonish knight who shows Harry, Ron, and Hermione how to get to the North Tower. For a time, he replaces the Fat Lady in the Gryffindor portrait hole.

Cho Chang: A pretty fourth-year Seeker for the Ravenclaw Quidditch team.

Penelope Clearwater: A Ravenclaw student and Percy Weasley's girlfriend.

Vincent Crabbe: One of Draco Malfoy's dimwitted cronies.

> "It's a mythic book. Harry himself is, in so many ways, an everyman. He comes from a dysfunctional family. Both his parents are dead. He's not a great student. I think many of us can relate to that. And yet he's capable of great things."
>
> **DAVID HEYMAN**, PRODUCER OF THE FILM
> *HARRY POTTER AND THE SORCERER'S STONE*

Colin Creevey: A second-year student at Hogwarts who is "deeply in awe of Harry."

Crookshanks: Hermione's cat. Crookshanks takes an instant dislike to Scabbers and helps Sirius Black get into the Gryffindor tower. He also helps the children follow Sirius by taming the Whomping Willow.

Davies: The captain of the Ravenclaw Quidditch team.

Dementors: Guards from Azkaban that can suck out souls and happiness.

Derek: Besides Harry, Ron, and Hermione, the only named student to remain at Hogwarts during the Christmas holidays.

Derrick: A Beater for the Slytherin Quidditch team.

Cedric Diggory: A fifth-year student in Hufflepuff and the new Seeker on the Hufflepuff Quidditch team. He is described by the girls as "tall," "good-looking," and "strong and silent."

J. K. Rowling

Albus Dumbledore: The wise, kind Headmaster of Hogwarts. He does not like having the dementors guard the school. He suggests to Hermione a method of saving Sirius and Buckbeak.

Dudley Dursley: Harry's fat, spoiled cousin.

Petunia Dursley: Harry's aunt. Mrs. Dursley neglects Harry while spoiling her own child, Dudley.

Vernon Dursley: Harry's cruel uncle. He makes a deal with Harry, promising to sign Harry's Hogsmeade permission form if Harry will behave himself during Aunt Marge's visit.

Errol: The Weasley family owl. Errol is old and decrepit.

Fang: Hagrid's pet boarhound.

The Fat Lady: The guardian of the Gryffindor portrait hole. Traumatized after an attack by Sirius Black, she takes a leave of absence.

Argus Filch: A bad-tempered Hogwarts caretaker.

Seamus Finnigan: A Gryffindor student. When Seamus faces the boggart, it takes the shape of a banshee.

Marcus Flint: The captain of the Slytherin Quidditch team.

Professor Flitwick: The Charms teacher at Hogwarts.

Florean Fortescue: The proprietor of an ice cream shop in Diagon Alley. He helps Harry with his homework.

Colonel Fubster: A retired man who tends to Aunt Marge's dogs while she is gone.

Cornelius Fudge: The Minister of Magic. He meets Harry at the Leaky Cauldron, overlooking Harry's illegal use of magic during the holidays.

Gregory Goyle: One of Draco Malfoy's dimwitted cronies.

Hermione Granger: A close friend of Harry's. She becomes estranged from Ron after a series of disagreements but reconciles with him eventually. Hermione deals with her heavy courseload by using a secret Time-Turner.

The Grim: A large black dog, said to be an omen of death. Harry thinks he has seen a Grim on several occasions, and Professor Trelawney sees one in Harry's tea leaves.

Davey Gudgeon: A Hogwarts student who was a classmate of Professor Lupin. Davey "nearly lost an eye" to the Whomping Willow shortly after it was planted.

Hagrid: The gamekeeper at Hogwarts and the new teacher of Care of Magical Creatures. Hagrid is discouraged when Buckbeak attacks Malfoy and spends the rest of the year teaching the students about mild, boring creatures.

Hermes: Percy Weasley's owl.

Hedwig: Harry's owl.

Madam Hooch: A Quidditch instructor who keeps an eye on Harry while he practices.

Angelina Johnson: A Chaser for the Gryffindor Quidditch team.

> "Getting children to read is no small blessing, and Rowling has provided them with a key to literacy. These are not, however, books for adults. Unlike *Huckleberry Finn* or *Alice in Wonderland*, the Potter series is not written on two levels, entertaining one generation while instructing another. Rather, it is in the category of Tom Swift and Dr. Dolittle; I was hooked on reading by them, but have laid aside my electric rifle and no longer talk to horses."
>
> **WILLIAM SAFIRE**

Lee Jordan: A Hogwarts student who provides play-by-play commentary for the Quidditch matches.

Professor Kettleburn: The retired teacher of Care of Magical Creatures.

Neville Longbottom: A third-year Gryffindor student who sleeps in Harry's dormitory. He writes down the Gryffindor password, causing problems when Sirius Black steals it for Crookshanks. Snape is especially cruel to Neville.

Remus J. Lupin: The new Defense Against the Dark Arts teacher. He dresses shabbily but is kind to Harry and seems learned in his field. He helps Harry learn to repel dementors.

J. K. Rowling

Ernie Macmillan: A student who has Muggle Studies class with Hermione.

Draco Malfoy: Harry's nemesis at Hogwarts. Draco teases Harry for fainting in the presence of dementors.

Lucius Malfoy: Draco's father. He uses his influence to see that Buckbeak is sentenced to death.

Macnair: An executioner sent by the Committee for the Disposal of Dangerous Creatures to kill Buckbeak. Macnair is a friend of Lucius Malfoy.

Aunt Marge: Vernon Dursley's sister. Marge behaves especially cruelly toward Harry. When she gets drunk and insults his parents, Harry causes her to swell up like a balloon.

Minerva McGonagall: The Transfiguration teacher at Hogwarts and Head of Gryffindor house. Strict McGonagall will not allow Harry to go to Hogsmeade without a signed permission form.

Montague: A Chaser for the Slytherin Quidditch team.

Nearly Headless Nick: A Gryffindor ghost.

Pansy Parkinson: A Slytherin girl who joins Malfoy in making fun of Harry.

Parvati Patil: A Hogwarts student. She is impressed by what she sees as the accuracy of Professor Trelawney's predictions.

Peeves: A troublemaking poltergeist. When Peeves tries to block a keyhole with gum, Lupin casts a spell that sends the wad of gum down Peeves's nostril.

Peter Pettigrew: A Hogwarts student who was a classmate of James Potter and Sirius Black. Peter was supposedly killed when Black blew up a street full of Muggles. We later discover that he is an Animagus.

Madam Pomfrey: The Hogwarts nurse. She is pleased at Lupin's supposed expertise.

Harry Potter: A thirteen-year-old wizard and the protagonist of the series. He believes Sirius Black is haunting him. Although Harry disregards the rules at times, he is willing to work hard, especially in his anti-dementor lessons.

Lily and James Potter: Harry's parents. Lily and James were murdered by Voldemort.

Ernie Prang: The driver of the Knight Bus.

Ripper: Aunt Marge's dog.

Madam Rosmerta: The barkeep at the Three Broomsticks pub.

Stan Shunpike: The conductor of the Knight Bus. He is the first to tell Harry about Sirius Black.

Severus Snape: The Potions master at Hogwarts and the Head of Slytherin house. Lupin and Sirius Black came close to killing Snape when they were all students. Snape tries to attack Sirius near the end of the book but is stopped by Harry, Ron, and Hermione.

The Sorting Hat: A battered talking wizard's hat that chooses houses for new Hogwarts students.

Alicia Spinnet: A Chaser for the Gryffindor Quidditch team.

Dean Thomas: A Gryffindor student. When Dean faces the boggart, it becomes a severed hand.

Tom: The proprietor of the Leaky Cauldron.

Sibyll Trelawney: The professor of Divination. Trelawney enjoys making predictions about students. On the first day of class, she sees an omen of Harry's death. Most of her predictions seem bogus, but she goes into a trance at year's end and predicts the return of Voldemort.

Professor Vector: A witch who teaches Arithmancy.

Voldemort: A Dark Lord whom Harry inadvertently defeated twelve years ago. Voldemort does not appear in this book, but one of his servants does.

Warrington: A Chaser for the Slytherin Quidditch team.

Arthur Weasley: The father of the Weasley children. He warns Harry not to chase after Sirius Black. Weasley is a major supporter of the Muggle Protection Act.

Bill Weasley: The oldest Weasley brother. Bill works in Egypt for a branch of Gringotts, the wizards' bank.

Charlie Weasley: The second oldest Weasley brother. Charlie studies dragons in Romania.

Fred and George Weasley: The Weasley twins. Fred and George love practical jokes. They give Harry the Marauder's Map, which they have stolen from Filch's office.

Ginny Weasley: The youngest Weasley child and a second-year student at Hogwarts. She has a crush on Harry.

Molly Weasley: The mother of the Weasley family. She argues that Harry should not be told the truth about Sirius Black.

Percy Weasley: The Head Boy and a stern enforcer of rules at Hogwarts.

Ron Weasley: Harry's best friend at Hogwarts. Ron becomes estranged from Hermione after a series of disagreements, and their rift pulls Harry away from Hermione. Eventually, Ron and Hermione reconcile.

Oliver Wood: The Captain of the Gryffindor Quidditch team. Wood, who is in his last year at Hogwarts, desperately wants to win the Quidditch Cup, which has eluded the Gryffindor team for seven years.

Reading *Harry Potter and the Prisoner of Azkaban*

Owl Post

Harry Potter is spending the summer with his aunt and uncle, **Petunia and Vernon Dursley**, and their fat son, **Dudley**. The Dursleys locked up Harry's books, but he picked the lock on the cupboard and retrieved them. **Ron Weasley** tried to call Harry, but Mr. Dursley hung up on him. **Hermione Granger** has not phoned. In the wee hours one morning, Harry realizes it is his thirteenth birthday.

Harry's owl, **Hedwig**, arrives. He and a Hogwarts owl are carrying **Errol**, the Weasleys' decrepit owl. Harry receives birthday notes and packages from Ron,

J. K. Rowling

"In many ways this installment seems to serve a transitional role in the seven-volume series: while many of the adventures are breathlessly relayed, they appear to be laying groundwork for even more exciting adventures to come. The beauty here lies in the genius of Rowling's plotting. Seemingly minor details established in books one and two unfold to take on unforeseen significance, and the finale, while not airtight in its internal logic, is utterly thrilling."

PUBLISHER'S WEEKLY REVIEW

Hermione, and **Hagrid**, the Hogwarts gamekeeper. In a note, Ron writes that his father, **Arthur Weasley**, won 700 Galleons in the *Daily Prophet* Grand Prize Galleon Draw. The family is spending most of the money on a vacation to Egypt. Ron has sent Harry a Pocket Sneakascope, which lights up and spins in the presence of someone untrustworthy. Hermione has sent him a broomstick servicing kit. Hagrid's package contains a book that seems to be alive. Harry has to chase the snapping book across the room and bind it shut with a belt.

Harry also receives a letter from **Professor McGonagall** with the list of books he will need for the upcoming school year. The letter contains a permission form that Harry must have signed by a guardian in order to visit the wizarding village of Hogsmeade with the other third-year students.

UNDERSTANDING AND INTERPRETING
Chapter One

Magic but Normal: The first and last sentences of Chapter One sum up Harry Potter's appeal. The chapter opens with the assertion, "Harry Potter was a highly unusual boy." The last sentence in the chapter begins with the words, "Extremely unusual though he was, at that moment Harry Potter felt just like everyone else." Harry Potter appeals to readers not only because of his magic powers, but because his normalcy dwarfs the exoticism of that magic. It is easy to identify with Harry, who might remind us of a normal kid with great talent at chess or soccer. Rowling assures us that Harry feels "just like everyone else," and that in spite of his skill, he is not snobby or hard to relate to.

A New Beginning: Like the first two novels in the series, this installment begins with Harry suffering under the abusive regime of his aunt and uncle. Rowling quickly reviews material most readers will remember from the previous books, sketching out Harry's career at Hogwarts, his relationship with the Dursleys, and the attack by Voldemort that killed his parents. At the end of the chapter, readers encounter a new twist. Instead of staying on the Hogwarts grounds, as usual, Harry will have an opportunity to visit the all-wizarding village of Hogsmeade.

CHAPTER TWO
Aunt Marge's Big Mistake

At breakfast, the Dursleys ignore Harry, as usual. Dudley eats and watches television news, which reports the escape of a convict named Black. Mr. Dursley tells Harry that **Aunt Marge** is coming for a weeklong visit. Harry remembers how cruel Marge has been to him on past visits. Vernon warns Harry not to pull any "*funny* stuff" during Marge's visit. Harry must pretend he is a student at St. Brutus's Secure Center for Incurably Criminal Boys. Harry strikes a deal with his uncle: he will behave for Marge if Mr. Dursley will sign the Hogsmeade permission form.

Marge arrives and makes cruel remarks to Harry. One night at dinner, when Marge compares Harry's family to dogs and says there was "something wrong with the bitch," her wineglass explodes in her hand. She attributes the mess to her firm grip, but Harry knows his uncontrollable anger broke the glass. On the last night of her visit, Marge, who has been drinking heavily, again insults Harry's parents, calling **Lily Potter** a "bad egg" and **James Potter** a "wastrel." Harry cannot contain his fury. He stands up for his parents, and after Marge calls him a "nasty liar," she swells up like a balloon and floats toward the ceiling.

Harry runs from the room and gathers his school things. Vernon tries to intercept him at the front door, but Harry threatens him with his wand and drags his trunk out into the night.

UNDERSTANDING AND INTERPRETING
Chapter Two

Key Details: Alert readers will know by now that Rowling uses details not only to enrich her stories, but to dole out important clues. In this chapter, the news report about the escaped criminal prompts a colorful display of Mr. Dursley's provincial mindset. Vernon rants about the criminal's appearance and the necessity of hanging ne'er-do-wells. The news report also provides the first mystery of the novel, prompting us to wonder who Black is, why he looks so unkempt, and why the newscaster fails to mention the facility where he was imprisoned.

New Initiative: Harry's method of escape shows his maturation. As in the first two volumes, Harry must escape from the Dursleys and return to Hogwarts. In the first novel, Hagrid rescues Harry. In the second novel, Ron comes to his window in a flying car. In this, the third novel, Harry shows more initiative than ever before by setting himself free. Harry used to bear up silently under insults to his mother, but now when Aunt Marge indirectly calls his mother a bitch, Harry feels he must act. Not only does he punish Marge by crushing her wineglass and puffing her up like a balloon, but he shows newfound initiative by grabbing his trunk and threatening his uncle with his wand.

CHAPTER THREE
The Knight Bus

Harry is convinced he will be expelled from Hogwarts for illegally doing magic during the summer holidays. He has decided to fly to London on his broomstick, hidden by his invisibility cloak, when he senses someone watching him. He sees a large shape lurking and quickly tries to get away, stumbling over his trunk. He throws out his wand hand to catch himself, and a triple-decker bus appears. **Stan Shunpike**, the conductor, explains that the Knight Bus is "emergency transport for the stranded witch or wizard." Harry boards the bus, falsely identifying himself as **Neville Longbottom** (another Hogwarts student). He is given a bed and meets the driver, **Ernie Prang**.

The bus appears and disappears with a loud bang, dropping off witches and wizards. Harry reads a newspaper story about **Sirius Black**, a wizard who escaped from Azkaban, the wizard prison. The Muggle Prime Minister was informed of his escape, which is why it was announced on the news. Stan tells Harry that Black was a supporter of Voldemort. After Voldemort lost his powers, his followers were rounded up. Black, cornered, blew up a street, killing a wizard and twelve Muggles.

The bus takes Harry to the Leaky Cauldron in London, where **Cornelius Fudge**, Minister of Magic, waits for him. Harry expects punishment, but Fudge says "no harm done" and says that Harry can stay at the Leaky Cauldron for the last two weeks before school. Harry finds this leniency odd, since he was severely reprimanded the previous year when a house-elf performed magic in the Dursley house. Fudge says only, "Circumstances change." Harry asks Fudge if he will sign Harry's Hogsmeade permission form, but Fudge says he cannot, since he is not Harry's parent or guardian. Harry finds Hedwig waiting for him in his room.

Chapter Three

Muggle and Magic: In this chapter, we learn that the Muggle world and the wizard world overlap, although the Muggles do not always realize it. Eerily, Harry finds himself momentarily caught in a space between the two worlds. Usually, he makes a seamless transition from the Dursley house to the magical world, but this time, he is stuck outside the house, miles away from Hogwarts or Diagon Alley. The presence of the huge black shape underlines the creepiness of lingering in this liminal place between Muggle and magic. The bus rescues Harry by providing him with a magical place. As the bus rumbles along, houses and street signs jump out of its way, demonstrating how the wizard world sometimes exists unnoticed alongside the Muggle world.

Rules and Regulations: In the Harry Potter series, the morality of rule-following is complex. Sometimes, authority figures reward the breaking of rules, usually when friendship or safety motivates the rule-breaking. However, this complex morality does not explain Fudge's leniency. As Harry knows, no real excuse exists for his behavior—he simply lost his temper. Marge provoked him, but he reacted with unacceptable violence. Fudge's excuses for Harry seem especially odd since Harry received a stern letter from the Ministry last year, castigating him for an incident that was not his fault. (Dobby, a house-elf, dropped a pudding and framed Harry for it.) Now, Fudge mysteriously cannot—or will not—explain why Harry will receive no punishment for his bad behavior.

CHAPTER FOUR
The Leaky Cauldron

Harry enjoys staying at the Leaky Cauldron and exploring Diagon Alley. He resists the temptation to buy the new Firebolt racing broom, but he does buy books and other school things. He discovers that the book Hagrid gave him, *The Monster Book of Monsters*, is required for his new Care of Magical Creatures class. While buying a book for his Divination class, he sees a book about death omens with a large black dog on it. The picture reminds him of the shape he saw in the dark on the night he ran away.

On the last day of the holidays, he meets up with Ron and Hermione. Ron has bought a new wand, and Hermione has three bags of books for the many new courses she will be taking. Hermione wants to buy an owl. Ron is worried

ARITHMANCY

One of the courses Hermione adds to her load is Arithmancy, the science of prediction using numbers and letters. Arithmancy was practiced by the ancient Greeks and by the ancient Chaldean peoples of Arabia. Its mathematical basis must have appealed to Hermione, who derides other, less scientific forms of divination.

about the health of his rat, **Scabbers**. In the Magical Menagerie, a witch sells Ron some rat tonic for Scabbers. A cat jumps onto Ron and chases Scabbers out of the shop. Harry and Ron retrieve Scabbers, and Hermione buys the cat, named **Crookshanks**.

The Weasleys, Harry, and Hermione have dinner together. **Fred and George** tease **Percy** about being Head Boy. After dinner, Harry overhears **Mr.** and **Mrs. Weasley** arguing about whether Harry should be told something. Harry hears them say that Sirius Black is after Harry Potter. Mr. Weasley wants to tell Harry so he can be alert. Mrs. Weasley thinks there is no point in scaring him. Guards from Azkaban will be watching over Hogwarts, though neither Mr. Weasley nor **Dumbledore** like the guards. Harry does not feel scared of Black.

UNDERSTANDING AND INTERPRETING

Chapter Four

Self-Control: Faced with Aunt Marge's abuse, Harry was not able to exercise self-control. He does possess a remarkable degree of restraint, however. He could certainly afford the Firebolt, which he wants more than he has wanted anything before, but he manages to resist buying it. Harry has a perfectly good broom, and he knows he must budget his money to last at least until the end of his Hogwarts career. Harry's ability to think beyond his immediate desires shows his increasing maturity.

Death and Dying: Harry Potter's story begins with the death of James and Lily, his parents. As the series progresses, death becomes an increasingly important element. At the end of *Harry Potter and the Sorcerer's Stone*, the destruction of the Sorcerer's Stone kills Dumbledore's friend, Nicolas Flamel. Starting in the middle of *Harry Potter and the Chamber of Secrets*, several Hogwarts students get Petrified, a state that is a gentler, less upsetting stand-in for death. In the third volume, death makes its earliest appearance yet. By the third chapter, Harry has seen an ominous figure he later identifies as an omen of death, a being supposedly out to get him. As the series progresses, Harry will come to a fuller understanding of death.

CHAPTER FIVE
The Dementor

At the station, Mr. Weasley begins to tell Harry about Black, but Harry says he already knows. Mr. Weasley asks Harry to promise not to "go *looking* for Black," regardless of what he hears. On the train, Harry, Ron, and, Hermione share a compartment with the sleeping **Professor Lupin**, a shabbily dressed man whom they assume is the new Defense Against the Dark Arts teacher. Harry tells his friends about Mr. Weasley's warning and the threat against him. Harry's Pocket Sneakascope spins and whines, foretelling the visit of **Draco Malfoy**, who stops by with his cohorts, **Vincent Crabbe** and **Gregory Goyle**. They back off when they see Professor Lupin in the compartment.

The train stops and the lights go out. In the darkness, **Neville Longbottom** and **Ginny Weasley** stumble into the compartment. Professor Lupin wakes up and conjures a light in his hands. A dark, cloaked figure appears in the doorway. The compartment turns icy, and Harry feels that he is "drowning in cold" and "being dragged downward." He hears distant screaming. The next thing he knows, he is lying on the floor, the lights are back on, and the train is moving.

Professor Lupin offers all the children chocolate and explains that the figure was a **dementor**, one of the Azkaban guards. Its presence made Harry pass out. Ron and Hermione say that Lupin told it to go and insisted none of them were hiding Sirius Black. When it did not leave, Lupin shot something silvery out of his wand and the dementor left. The children eat their chocolate and feel warm again.

At Hogwarts, Malfoy teases Harry for fainting. **McGonagall** takes Harry and Hermione to her office. She is concerned for Harry's well-being. **Madam Pomfrey** says Harry should have some chocolate, and he says he has already had some. Harry steps outside while Hermione talks to McGonagall about her course schedule.

At the welcoming feast, Dumbledore says that the school is now guarded by dementors, and no one can leave without permission. He introduces Lupin and the other addition to the faculty, Hagrid, who will be teaching Care of Magical Creatures. In the dormitory that night, Harry feels like he is back at home.

UNDERSTANDING AND INTERPRETING
Chapter Five

Dividing Dialogue: As Ron and Hermione talk about Hogsmeade, they reveal familiar aspects of their personalities. Ron talks almost exclusively about the candy shop, suggesting his carefree nature and his delight in the simple pleasures of childhood. Hermione talks about the history of the village, as befits her

DEMENTORS

In an interview with the *Times* of London, Rowling explained that dementors represent depression. "Depression is the most unpleasant thing I have ever experienced. It is that absence of being able to envisage that you will ever be cheerful again, the absence of hope, that very deadened feeling, which is so very different from feeling sad."

intellectualism. Additionally, the progress of their conversation points to the rift that will develop between them. They hardly seem to hear each other as the conversation progresses, voicing their own thoughts without listening to each other. Ron's rat, Scabbers, and Hermione's cat, Crookshanks, take an instant dislike to each other, prefiguring their masters' impending separation.

Passed Out, Singled Out: Once again, Harry finds himself singled out, this time for an embarrassing reason. In the beginning, students whispered about Harry because of his fame. Now, they whisper about him because he is the only student who faints at the sight of a dementor. Harry, who disliked the attention he got for his babyhood deeds, feels equally uncomfortable about getting attention for his dramatic reaction to dementors.

CHAPTER SIX
Talons and Tea Leaves

Ron cannot understand Hermione's class schedule, which requires her to attend three lessons at once. Hermione will only say she has "fixed it all with Professor McGonagall." With help from a clumsy knight named **Sir Cadogan**, who lives in one of the paintings, the students find their way to the top of the North Tower, where Professor Trelawney will teach Divination. Trelawney likes making predictions about students. She says "around Easter one of our number will leave us forever" and predicts whatever Lavender Brown is dreading will happen on October 16. As they prepare to read tea leaves, Trelawney correctly predicts that Neville will break a teacup. She picks up Harry's saucer of leaves and sees the Grim—a giant dog and "the worst omen"—of *death*.

In Transfiguration, McGonagall discusses Animagi—"wizards who could transform at will into animals." To illustrate the process, she transforms herself into a cat. The impassive class, still traumatized from Trelawney's predictions, does not react to her feat. McGonagall eases their minds by explaining that each year Trelawney predicts the death of a student, but no one has ever died.

GRIM DOG ✹ The Grim, a phantom black dog, has appeared in English folklore for centuries under many names. It is often a portent of death or disaster. The "Church Grim" or "Kirk Grim" was said to guard the dead in churchyards, keeping them from the devil. One of the most famous fictional appearances of these dogs occurs in Sir Arthur Conan Doyle's novel *The Hound of the Baskervilles*.

The **HIPPOGRIFF** is a legendary creature often found in ancient Greek art and later used as a symbol of love. It is the offspring of a male griffin and a female horse. The Middle Ages poet Ludovico Ariosto wrote in his epic *Orlando Furioso* that the knights of Charlemagne used hippogriffs as steeds.

At lunch, Harry tells his friends that the night he ran away, he saw the black dog. Ron and Hermione argue about the accuracy of Divination. The next class is Care of Magical Creatures, which the Gryffindors have with the Slytherins. Hagrid introduces the class to hippogriffs, creatures with the back of a horse and the front of an eagle. He tells them they must never insult the creatures. Harry volunteers to meet Buckbeak, a hippogriff. He bows to Buckbeak, who bows in return and allows Harry to climb onto him for a short, uncomfortable flight around the paddock. The other students follow Harry's example with their hippogriffs, but Malfoy insults Buckbeak, who attacks him, badly cutting his arm.

That evening, Harry, Ron, and Hermione go to see Hagrid, who is drunk and convinced he will be fired because of the hippogriff's attack. They try to cheer him up. Hagrid gets angry with Harry for leaving the castle after dark.

UNDERSTANDING AND INTERPRETING
Chapter Six

Discord over Divination: The rift opening between Ron and Hermione widens after Divination class. Hermione casts aspersions on Trelawney's ability to see the future, calling Divination "a lot of guesswork." Hermione shares this opinion with McGonagall, who scoffs at Trelawney's predictions. Ron seems taken with Divination and makes a convincing argument by telling Hermione, "You just don't like being bad at something for a change." The quarrel is particularly painful because Hermione and Ron are both right in their own way.

Care of Magical Creatures: Hagrid has been marginalized in the wizarding world, particularly in the Hogwarts community, ever since Tom Riddle falsely accused him of opening the Chamber of Secrets fifty years ago. In the previous novel in the series, Harry, Ron, and Hermione vindicated Hagrid, restoring his standing. Dumbledore always believed in Hagrid's innocence and now makes him a teacher. For the first time in years, Hagrid gets the respect he deserves. The newness of this respect makes it all the more painful when Malfoy turns against Hagrid just as Tom Riddle did fifty years earlier. Malfoy's provocations convince

Hagrid that, once again, a student will make false accusations and cause his downfall. For the time being, Malfoy does not possess the dangerous power of Tom Riddle, though the parallels between the two are clear.

CHAPTER SEVEN
The Boggart in the Wardrobe

In Potions class, Malfoy pretends his injury has rendered his arm useless. Snape makes Harry and Ron prepare Malfoy's ingredients. Malfoy brags that his father's influence will probably get Hagrid fired. Seamus Finnegan mentions that Sirius Black was sighted near Hogwarts. Malfoy says if he were Harry he would "be out there looking for him" because he would "want revenge." Snape tries out Neville's shrinking potion on Neville's toad, **Trevor**, and turns Trevor into a tadpole. Snape restores the toad but takes five points from Gryffindor, saying Hermione helped Neville with the potion. On the way upstairs, Hermione disappears, then reappears, without explanation.

Professor Lupin takes his Defense Against the Dark Arts students to the staff-room. On the way, he casts a spell on the rude Peeves. Snape insults Neville's abilities and then leaves the staffroom. The students see the wardrobe move, and Lupin explains there is a boggart in it. Hermione says a boggart changes shape, turning into whatever its viewer fears most. Harry realizes that crowds might stymie the boggart, since it will not know which fear to embody. Lupin tells his students that laughter will defeat a boggart. He teaches the students a spell and tells them to imagine what frightens them most and then try to make that thing seem ridiculous. Harry thinks of a dementor but cannot find a way to make it funny.

Lupin asks Neville to stand in front of the wardrobe and then releases the boggart, which comes out in the shape of Professor Snape. When Neville casts his spell, the professor is suddenly dressed in Neville's grandmother's clothes. Other students take turns wearing down the boggart. For Ron, the boggart becomes a giant spider, which loses its legs after Ron performs the spell. Lupin steps in front of Harry, taking

SHAPE SHIFTERS The boggart is a figure from Northern English folklore. Some legends describe boggarts as shape shifters, others as beings that inhabit houses. Boggarts are mischievous and frightening, but not usually dangerous. They delight in causing small accidents and playing pranks around the household.

Harry's turn for him. For Lupin, the boggart becomes a "silvery white orb." He lets Neville finish off the boggart with laughter.

Lupin awards points to the students who faced the boggart and to Harry and Hermione for answering questions. Harry wonders why Lupin did not let him face the boggart.

UNDERSTANDING AND INTERPRETING
Chapter Seven

Smart but Suspect: As we know from the first two novels in the series, Defense Against the Dark Arts teachers are not what they seem and have an uncanny tendency to last no more than a year in their position. Lupin, the new Defense Against the Dark Arts teacher, seems trustworthy and smart. Ron calls Lupin's first class the best they have ever had in the subject. But Rowling plants seeds of doubt about Lupin, and precedent tells us that his teaching post makes him suspect. Significant details include the name Lupin, which means wolf in Latin, and the mysterious orb, the object Lupin fears most.

CHAPTER EIGHT
Flight of the Fat Lady

Harry loves Lupin's classes and detests Snape's classes. One day, he learns that the first Hogsmeade weekend will be on Halloween and decides to ask McGonagall if he can go. In the common room, Crookshanks tries to attack Scabbers, which prompts another argument between Ron and Hermione.

On October 16, Lavender Brown hears that a fox has killed her pet rabbit. Lavender interprets this incident as proof of Trelawney's skill. Trelawney predicted that on October 16, whatever Lavender most dreads would happen. Hermione points out that Lavender could not have dreaded the death of a baby bunny and says that the attack did not even happen on the sixteenth. Harry asks McGonagall if he can go to Hogsmeade, but she says no.

While the others are in Hogsmeade, Harry tires of the younger students in the common room and wanders the halls. He eventually meets Lupin, who invites him into his office for a cup of tea. Lupin explains that he kept Harry from the boggart because he assumed that Harry was most afraid of Voldemort and worried that the appearance of the Dark Lord would cause the students to panic. Lupin uses Voldemort's name, which impresses Harry. Harry admits that he fears dementors more than he fears Voldemort, which impresses Lupin. "[W]hat you fear most of all is—fear," Lupin says.

Snape comes in and gives Lupin a potion to drink. Lupin tells Harry he has been feeling "off-color," and Snape's potion is "the only thing that helps." When Ron and Hermione return from Hogsmeade, Harry tells them about the potion. They wonder if Snape covets the Defense Against the Dark Arts job and wants to kill Lupin.

After the Halloween feast, the Gryffindors try to go to their common room, but the Fat Lady is missing from the portrait that covers the entrance. The painting has been slashed. Dumbledore sends McGonagall to find the Fat Lady. Peeves says that the damage to the painting was caused by Sirius Black.

UNDERSTANDING AND INTERPRETING
Chapter Eight

The Likeable Lupin: Rowling establishes Lupin's unique attitude toward his students by showing him riding the Hogwarts Express, something no other teacher does. Harry enjoys a comfortable, respectful relationship with Lupin that is unlike his relationship with any other teacher at Hogwarts. Lupin's willingness to treat his students as peers makes him a favorite. While Lupin is certainly in charge of his class, he tempers his authority with respect. He works with his students, a technique very different from Snape's adversarial brand of teaching. Having tea with Lupin gives Harry a chance to talk privately and honestly with his teacher. We have seen Harry alone in the offices of other teachers, interactions which are usually formal and a bit uncomfortable. Alone in Lupin's office, Harry is relaxed. He even asks about the boggart and receives a frank explanation for why Lupin did not let Harry face the beast. Harry's willingness to speak his mind contrasts with an episode in the previous novel in which, even after prompting, Harry declined to tell Dumbledore about the voice he had been hearing.

Nearing Doom: True to form, Rowling raises the stakes as the novel progresses, making each episode more fraught with meaning. Sirius Black creeps closer to the students. In Chapter Eight, he breaks through an invisible barrier. No longer an abstract threat to the outside world, he has penetrated the students' home, leaving a physical mark of his presence. Black has gradually changed from a figure half-noticed by Harry on the Muggle news to a murderous wizard who breaches the Gryffindor common room.

CHAPTER NINE
Grim Defeat

The students sleep in the Great Hall while the teachers search the school for Sirius. Harry hears Snape telling Dumbledore that he thinks Black had "inside help." Snape pointedly reminds Dumbledore that he objected to a certain hiring decision, but Dumbledore interrupts Snape before he can point the finger at Lupin.

A portrait of Sir Cadogan takes the place of the Fat Lady. McGonagall calls Harry to her office. She is surprised that Harry already knows Black is after him. Initially McGonagall asks Harry to give up Quidditch practice, but when he protests, she agrees to let him continue under the supervision of Madam Hooch. Right before the next Quidditch match, Slytherin claims Malfoy's arm is still hurt and their team can't play. Gryffindor will play Hufflepuff in the upcoming Quidditch match, facing Hufflepuff's new Seeker, Cedric Diggory.

Snape teaches class for Lupin, who is feeling ill. He criticizes Lupin and announces that he will teach about werewolves. When Hermione answers a question without being called on, Snape takes five points from Gryffindor and calls Hermione an "insufferable know-it-all," reducing her to tears. Ron challenges Snape, asking why he asked the question if he did not want to be told the answer. Snape gives him detention.

Peeves wakes Harry early on the morning of the match. The weather at the Quidditch match is horrible, and the rain on Harry's glasses obscures his vision. When Wood calls a timeout, Hermione casts a water-repelling spell on Harry's glasses. Harry spies a large black dog in the stadium, but when he looks again, it is gone. Wood calls to Harry, who turns to see Diggory heading toward the Snitch. Harry dives for it, but as he drops, he feels cold and sees dementors below him. He hears a woman screaming, "Not Harry. . . kill me instead," and then he hears shrill laughter.

Harry wakes in the hospital wing, surrounded by his friends. They explain that he fell off his broom and plummeted fifty feet to the ground below. Everyone thought he had died. Dumbledore slowed Harry's fall and banished the dementors, using something silver from his wand. Diggory caught the Snitch before he realized that Harry had fallen. He tried to call off the match, but it was too late. Gryffindor lost, and Harry's broom went flying into the Whomping Willow, which angrily smashed it to bits.

UNDERSTANDING AND INTERPRETING
Chapter Nine

Standing Up to Snape: In part, the Harry Potter series is about the intellectual and emotional progress of children. Rowling uses many subtle devices to show the children moving from early adolescence to early adulthood. Harry, Parvati, Hermione, and Ron talk back to Snape in a way they never would have in their first year at Hogwarts. As experienced students, they do not automatically accept Snape's declarations and instructions as gospel. Snape's bullying does not intimidate them as it used to, and they willingly stand up for what they feel is just, even at the risk of incurring punishment. When Ron receives detention for defending Hermione, he does not regret his actions. He knows that Snape was being cruel to Hermione, and he is not ashamed of telling him so.

A Formula for Fiction: Chapter Nine marks a low point for Harry. He panics when faced with dementors, loses a Quidditch game for the first time, and sees his beloved broomstick in pieces. Quidditch has been a safe haven for Harry, the only arena in which he felt absolutely confident of success. It humiliates him to lose at Quidditch, and it disturbs him that his fear of dementors caused the loss. The loss may dishearten Harry, but it puts him on a classic trajectory. As we know from nearly all movies about sports, typically the hero or heroes must suffer humiliating losses before battling back to achieve victory. Harry has been consistently victorious in his sport, which would seem to rule out the " Rocky"-style plot, but in Chapter Nine, Rowling hands Harry a loss and begins remaking him as a vulnerable sports weakling.

CHAPTER TEN
The Marauder's Map

Harry has told no one about the appearance of the Grim in the stadium. He now realizes that, in the presence of the dementors, he hears the final pleas his mother made before dying. Lupin returns to class and cancels Snape's assignment of an essay on werewolves. After class, he explains to Harry that dementors suck all the good feelings and memories from people. They affect Harry so severely because his worst memories are more terrifying than everyone else's. Lupin agrees to give Harry anti-dementor lessons next term.

As the other students leave for another Hogsmeade trip, Fred and George waylay Harry and give him the Marauder's Map, which they stole from Filch's office during their first year. When used properly, the map shows Hogwarts, secret passages and all. It also shows the location of every person in the school, making it easy to avoid teachers. Harry uses the map to take a secret passage to Honeyduke's sweets shop in Hogsmeade, where he meets Ron and Hermione. The three go to the Three Broomsticks for butterbeer.

McGonagall, Flitwick, Hagrid, and Cornelius Fudge enter, and Harry hides under the table. They discuss the history of Sirius Black, and Harry secretly eavesdrops. Black was James Potter's best friend at Hogwarts, the best man at James's and Lily's wedding, and Harry's godfather. When Voldemort was hunting the Potters, they used a Fidelius Charm to conceal their whereabouts. The charm works by concealing a secret inside a Secret-Keeper—Black, in the Potters' case. The secret can be discovered only if the Secret-Keeper willingly reveals it. Apparently, Black revealed the Potters' secret, betraying them to Voldemort. When Voldemort lost his power trying to kill Harry, Hagrid arrived to take the baby away and met Black, who seemed upset. Black asked to keep Harry but eventually relented and gave Hagrid his beloved flying motorcycle. Shortly after that, Peter Pettigrew, who had worshipped Black and Potter at Hogwarts, cornered Black on a Muggle street. Pettigrew did not draw his wand fast enough, and Black blasted him and much of the street, killing a dozen Muggles. Fudge visited Black on his last trip to Azkaban, the island fortress where dementors guard wizard prisoners. Most prisoners are mumbling shells of their former selves, but Black seemed rational and calm. The teachers leave, and Ron and Hermione gaze speechlessly at Harry.

UNDERSTANDING AND INTERPRETING
Chapter Ten

A Legacy of Betrayal: As Harry grows older, he learns more about his parents' deaths. Most of this new information is thrust upon him, as when he hears his mother's anguished screams during the Quidditch match, and here when he listens to the adults discuss Sirius Black. Harry has not actively sought out facts about his parents' death. He has not approached Dumbledore, for example, and asked to talk about the past. Increasingly, however, Harry's passive attitude toward the past is becoming untenable. He now hears that Sirius Black betrayed his parents, and it seems he must take some stand against Black, his own godfather, especially since the betrayer is now threatening him.

Facing the Demons: Harry actively attempts to thwart his personal demons. As usual, he shows a willingness to face what frightens him most. When Harry talks with Lupin about the dementors, he is eager to learn how to combat them. Many other characters in the novel run away from problems or find ways of avoiding confrontation. Harry's instincts are different. He plans not to hide from the dementors or to run away from them, but to fight them.

CHAPTER ELEVEN
The Firebolt

Back in his dormitory, Harry finds his parents' wedding picture in his photo album. He sees their best man, the person he now knows to be Sirius Black. Harry feels intense hatred for Black. The next morning, the holidays begin. Harry finally tells Ron and Hermione about hearing his mother's screams whenever a dementor is near. Hermione begs him not to seek revenge on Black. Ron says that when Peter Pettigrew was killed, all that was left of him was a finger.

The three go to visit Hagrid. He is sobbing, distraught at Lucius Malfoy's move to have Buckbeak tried before the Committee for the Disposal of Dangerous Creatures. Hagrid fears for Buckbeak's life. The students agree to help with the hippogriff's defense.

On Christmas morning, Harry receives a Firebolt racing broom with no card or signature. Hermione cautions him against riding it. Hermione brings Crookshanks into the boys' dormitory, and Ron tries to kick the cat to keep him away from Scabbers. Harry's Pocket Sneakascope whistles and spins. Ron and Hermione are miffed at each other because of the conflict between their pets. Scabbers looks sick.

At lunch, the six students staying at Hogwarts for the holidays sit at a table with several teachers. Lupin, ill again, is absent. Snape says he has concocted "the potion" for Lupin. After lunch Hermione stays behind to talk to McGonagall. Later, McGonagall and Hermione arrive in the Gryffindor common room. Hermione has told McGonagall about the Firebolt, and McGonagall insists on confiscating it and checking it for jinxes, a process that will take several weeks. Ron is furious with Hermione. She says she thinks the broom is a gift from Sirius Black.

UNDERSTANDING AND INTERPRETING
Chapter Eleven

For Your Own Good: When McGonagall confiscates Harry's broom, she delivers a variation of the phrase all children occasionally hear from adults: "I'm doing this for your own good." Coming from McGonagall, this assurance is expected. Coming from Hermione, it is infuriating. Good-intentioned Hermione sneaks around behind Harry's back, ratting him out to McGonagall. She does what she thinks best for Harry, but by acting like an adult authority, urging Harry and Ron to follow the rules, and betraying them to teachers, she distances herself from her friends. In some ways, Hermione is more like McGonagall than she is like Harry and Ron, and her intelligence and maturity occasionally put her in difficult situations. Hermione usually obeys her nature and conscience, which can land her on the wrong side of her peers.

Christmas Crackers: The Harry Potter novels have a tinge of exoticism for American readers since they involve unfamiliar British traditions. This chapter, for example, makes reference to Christmas crackers, decorated tubes of cardboard with a small slip of paper protruding from each end. When the slips are pulled, these tubes make a loud cracking noise. Christmas crackers usually contain prizes and silly paper hats, which the assembled revelers don. Rowling uses the Christmas cracker tradition to humorous effect. When Snape opens his cracker, he finds a hat reminiscent of the one the boggart wore for Neville.

CHAPTER TWELVE
The Patronus

Ron and Harry are angry with Hermione for telling McGonagall about the Firebolt. They notice that Lupin "[s]till looks ill." Hermione says it is obvious what is wrong with him. She acts superior, Ron snaps at her, and the conversation ends badly.

At the first anti-dementor lesson, Lupin shows Harry how to conjure a Patronus, a shield against dementors that is "a kind of positive force, a projection of the very things a dementor feeds upon." To do this advanced charm, Harry must concentrate on a happy memory. Lupin has brought a boggart so Harry can practice. He releases the boggart, which takes the form of a dementor. Harry concentrates on his first flight on a broomstick, but again he hears his mother's screams and passes out. When he comes to, he insists on continuing the lesson. This time, he thinks of Gryffindor winning the house cup. He hears a man's voice, he assumes his father's, telling Lily, "Take Harry and go. . . . I'll hold him off." On his third effort, Harry recalls the moment he found out he was a wizard. He succeeds in conjuring a weak Patronus that holds off the dementor. He watches Lupin change the boggart into a silver ball and return it to its box. Harry asks Lupin if he knew Sirius Black, and Lupin says he did.

Harry and Ron wonder how Hermione gets to all of her classes, some of which seem to be simultaneous. Harry continues to struggle in his anti-dementor lessons. Lupin tells him about the dementors' ultimate weapon, the Dementor's Kiss. By wielding this weapon, the creatures can suck the soul out of their victims. Lupin tells Harry that the dementors will do that to Black. Harry says Black deserves it.

McGonagall returns the Firebolt, which is now thoroughly inspected. Harry and Ron decide to make up with Hermione. Harry approaches her and starts a conversation about school, but moments later, Ron rushes in, clutching a bloody sheet and a few cat hairs. It seems Crookshanks has finally eaten Scabbers.

UNDERSTANDING AND INTERPRETING
Chapter Twelve

Personal Triumph: When Harry learns that he must think of happy memories in order to conjure up a Patronus, his choice of memories indicates his maturity level. Harry is thirteen, and unsurprisingly, the happy memories he summons up are self-involved moments of personal triumph. He thinks of winning the house cup, discovering his natural talent for flying, and realizing he is superior to his oppressors, the Dursleys. None of these memories succeeds in conjuring a strong Patronus. Their failure suggests that Harry must rely on a different sort of memory if he wants to defeat the dementors.

Circumstantial Evidence: In each of the novels so far, Harry and his friends have made incorrect assumptions based on circumstantial evidence—assumptions that have hampered their ability to discern the truth. In this chapter, they misread clues once again, assuming that Crookshanks has eaten Scabbers. They should know from past experience that in their world the simple explanation is rarely the correct one. Eventually they will see parallels between the false accusation of Crookshanks and the false accusation of Sirius Black. The misunderstanding about Crookshanks and Scabbers foreshadows the crucial incorrect assumption the friends have made.

CHAPTER THIRTEEN
Gryffindor Versus Ravenclaw

Ron and Hermione are furious with each other, and Hermione accuses Harry of taking Ron's side. The friendship seems to be over. Meanwhile, Harry's new Firebolt helps him have a great practice. Afterward, he lets Ron fly the broom.

On the way back to the castle, Harry sees a pair of eyes. Fearing the Grim, he conjures some light and realizes it is only Crookshanks.

The Gryffindors' next match is against Ravenclaw. On the way to the match, Malfoy teases Harry about the dementor. Harry scoffs at Malfoy's substandard Seeker ability. He puts his wand under his Quidditch robes, in case the dementors return. Harry notices the Ravenclaw Seeker, **Cho Chang**, who is "extremely pretty." Harry nearly catches the Snitch early in the match, but a Bludger drives him off course. The second time he sees the Snitch, Cho blocks him. Harry throws Cho off course by pretending to see the Snitch and diving. Then he really does see the Snitch high in the air and races after it, well ahead of Cho. He looks down, sees three dementors, and conjures a Patronus, a large "silvery white" material that shoots from the end of his wand. He grabs the Snitch, winning the game. It excites Harry to realize that the dementors had no effect on him, but then he discovers that his tormenters were only Malfoy and his Slytherin cronies disguised as dementors. McGonagall gives the offenders detention and takes fifty points from Slytherin.

In Gryffindor tower, the victors hold a celebratory party, which Hermione does not attend. Harry tries to convince Ron to forgive her, but he will not. That night, Ron wakes and sees Sirius Black standing over him with a knife. When he screams, Black disappears. Sir Cadogan admits to letting a man into the tower—a man who read the password from a piece of paper. Neville admits that the paper was his.

UNDERSTANDING AND INTERPRETING
Chapter Thirteen

Violence and Lust: Harry, older now than he was when the series began, begins to experience feelings of violence and lust. In Chapter Twelve, Harry admits to a hatred of Sirius Black so intense that he believes Black deserves to have his soul sucked out by a dementor. In Chapter Thirteen, Harry sees Cho on the Quidditch field and feels "a slight lurch in the region of his stomach." Rowling coyly alludes to "the region of his stomach" as if to underline Harry's emerging sexuality.

Cranky and Unkind: In previous volumes, the halfway point marked the place at which Harry, Ron, and Hermione begin to work together to solve a mystery. The halfway point in this volume, however, has Ron and Hermione estranged from one another and Harry caught uncomfortably in the middle of their quarrel. Rowling's change in formula serves two purposes. First, it is a device. By veering off the beaten path, the novel engages us and fends off accusations of predictability. Second, it is a development that comes organically from the characters. Harry,

Ron, and Hermione have been friends for years now. Familiarity can breed crankiness and unkindness. Ron is sick of Hermione's superior attitude, and she is fed up with his dimness. The quarrel that ensues is a realistic development in a long friendship.

CHAPTER FOURTEEN
Snape's Grudge

Hagrid invites Harry and Ron to tea. He scolds them for treating Hermione badly. She has been visiting Hagrid to help with Buckbeak's case, and he sees her sadness and loneliness.

Harry talks with Ron about sneaking into Hogsmeade with the other students next weekend. Hermione overhears them and threatens to tell McGonagall about the Marauder's Map if Harry goes. Harry ignores her and uses the map and the invisibility cloak to sneak into the village. He and Ron buy lots of wizarding jokes in a shop called Zonko's and then go to look at the Shrieking Shack, the "most haunted dwelling in Britain." Malfoy, Crabbe, and Goyle appear and insult Ron. Harry, hidden by the cloak, throws mud at them. The cloak slips, and Malfoy sees Harry's face.

Harry rushes back to school, leaving the cloak in the secret passage. Snape, tipped off by Malfoy, apprehends him. Snape tells Harry he is just like his father, an "exceedingly arrogant" rule-breaker. When Snape says that James's head was swollen, Harry snaps and yells at him to shut up. Harry says his father saved Snape's life. Snape sneers at Harry, informing him that James Potter only "saved" him by backing out of a practical joke that would have killed Snape.

When Snape tries to make the Marauder's Map show him its secrets, insults from Moony, Prongs, Padfoot, and Wormtail, the makers of the map, appear on the parchment. Snape mysteriously summons Lupin and asks him about the parchment, accusing Harry of getting it "directly from the manufacturers." Lupin says it is probably a joke parchment that insults whoever reads it. Ron arrives, trying to cover for Harry. Lupin takes the boys away, apparently to discuss an essay.

Once in private, Lupin explains that he knows the parchment is a map stolen from Filch. He takes it from Harry, saying he knows the makers. Lupin reminds Harry that his parents died to save his life, and taking risks by going into Hogsmeade insults their sacrifice. Later, Hermione approaches the boys. Ron accuses her of coming to gloat, but she says that Buckbeak was convicted and will be executed.

Chapter Fourteen

Cavalier Harry: Snape is undoubtedly distasteful, but some of his gripes with Harry have merit. Harry's attitude toward authority is increasingly cavalier. Previously, he broke rules to save Muggles from persecution or to stop Voldemort from achieving immortality. No similarly lofty project excuses his current behavior. He has become a bit cocky, breaking rules solely for his own enjoyment. It is unfair that the Dursleys refused to sign a permission slip for Hogsmeade, but nothing truly compelling demands Harry's presence at Hogsmeade. He simply enjoys going and refuses to let rules spoil his fun. When Harry arrives in Hogsmeade, he buys wizarding jokes and throws mud at other students—childish behavior that compromises his disguise. Most importantly, Harry puts his life at risk by straying from the protection of Hogwarts and putting himself at Black's mercy. Snape understands all of this, but Harry loathes Snape and cannot listen to him, even when he speaks reason. He does respond, however, to Lupin's gentle reprimands.

Adolescent Angst: Along with his disregard for rules, Harry picks up several of the less pleasant hallmarks of adolescence. He cuts off Hermione with ease, fails to make a real effort to reconcile with her, neglects Hagrid completely in his preparations to save Buckbeak, and mutters sullenly to adults. Harry, in realistic fashion, becomes more selfish and self-centered as he enters his teenage years.

CHAPTER FIFTEEN
The Quidditch Final

Hermione shows Harry and Ron a tear-streaked note from Hagrid. She says there will be an appeal, but Lucius Malfoy has intimidated the Committee. Ron tells Hermione that she will not have to work on the appeal alone; he will help. Hermione, weeping, says she is sorry about Scabbers. The friends reconcile. Malfoy sees Hagrid crying over Buckbeak and calls him pathetic. Hermione slaps Malfoy and draws her wand, scaring off the bullies. Ron is impressed.

Hermione misses Charms class and lunch. The boys find her asleep in the common room. Upset and flustered, she insists she is not "trying to do too much." In Divination class, Trelawney introduces crystal balls. Harry and Ron cannot see anything in theirs. Trelawney looks into Harry's and sees the Grim. Hermione finds this ridiculous, but Trelawney says that Hermione's mind is "hopelessly mundane." Stunning everyone, Hermione quits class on the spot and storms out. Lavender worshipfully points out that Hermione has fulfilled Trelawney's prophecy that one of the class would "leave us forever" around Easter.

On the eve of the Quidditch final against Slytherin, Harry can't sleep. Outside on the lawn, he sees Crookshanks and a large black dog. The next day Cho wishes Harry good luck, making him blush. The Slytherin team uses violent and illegal tactics in the Quidditch match, resulting in several penalty goals for Gryffindor. To capture the Quidditch Cup, Gryffindor must win the match by more than 200 points, which means Harry cannot catch the Snitch until his team leads by at least sixty points. Harry succeeds in luring Malfoy away from the Snitch until Gryffindor has a big lead. When Harry spots the Snitch near the ground, Malfoy is already far ahead of him, but Harry catches up, blocks Malfoy with one arm, and catches the Snitch with his other hand. Gryffindor wins the Quidditch Cup.

UNDERSTANDING AND INTERPRETING
Chapter Fifteen

Unearthing Passions: Harry discovered a natural talent when he first mounted a broom. Other characters in the novel do not discover their inclinations quite as rapidly as Harry, but gradually they begin to understand where their skills lie. In Divination, Parvati and Lavender flourish. They respect Trelawney and her predictions and want to follow in her footsteps. Hermione, on the other hand, thinks Divination is rubbish. Her hatred of Divination is actually a boon. It throws her true academic passions into high relief and makes her realize that she must focus her energy. Trying to be the best student in every subject, including those subjects she scorns, is a pointless waste of time. Quitting Divination marks a major turning point for Hermione. From this moment on, she can concentrate on what she loves and discard the rest.

Dirty and Clean: The two teams' different styles of Quidditch play reflect their different personalities. The Slytherins play a dirty game, knocking players from their broomsticks, grabbing Gryffindor heads instead of the Quidditch balls, and trying to hurt Harry in the week before the game. The Slytherins have expensive broomsticks, but they do not have adequate flying skills. Their team does not have a single female member, whereas the Gryffindors are a mix of boys and girls. Gryffindor plays fairly and retaliates hard. They make up for their inexpensive brooms through rigorous practice. The greatest difference between the two rivaling houses, as symbolized by the rival Quidditch teams, is work ethic. Gryffindor works hard to succeed, and Slytherin feels that success should fall into their laps. They would rather work hard at sabotaging the other team's chances for success than honing their own skills.

SIBYLL, A SIBYL

Professor Trelawney's first name, Sibyll, fits her perfectly. In ancient times, it was believed that some women, called sibyls, were oracles who could predict the future. The usage of the word "sibyl" dates back to at least 500 B.C. A sibyl appears in *The Aeneid*.

Some Christian writers believed that sibyls were holy prophets. By the Middle Ages, Christians identified twelve sibyls as prophets of God's word.

CHAPTER SIXTEEN
Professor Trelawney's Prediction

Everyone busily prepares for exams. Hermione is scheduled to take two exams at once. She will not explain to Ron how this is possible. Harry receives a note from Hagrid, saying that Buckbeak's appeal will take place at Hogwarts on the last day of exams. An executioner will come to the school.

The students take their exams. Hagrid, depressed, gives an extremely easy exam that involves tending flobberworms, which require no tending. Lupin creates an obstacle course with various dangerous creatures. Harry defeats the boggart and earns a high score. In the middle of the day, Cornelius Fudge arrives with **Macnair**, the executioner, and a member of the Committee for the Disposal of Dangerous Creatures.

Students take the Divination exam one at a time. Harry goes last. He sees nothing in the crystal ball, but he lies and says he sees Buckbeak being set free. Trelawney seems disappointed that Harry does not see the animal's death. As Harry starts to leave, Trelawney goes into a trance and says that the servant of the Dark Lord will "break free and set out to rejoin his master" before midnight. She says that the Dark Lord will return "greater and more terrible than ever." When Trelawney comes out of the trance, she says she must have dozed off, and indignantly tells Harry that she would never predict something as "far-fetched" as the return of Voldemort.

> "The Harry Potter series are a way of escape, a way to free the mind from boundaries, without hitting the nerves in a wrong way. His story has a way of putting you in his shoes. You're there with him in his head, through his entire journey."
>
> **NINA HUSS**, FROM THE ONLINE COLUMN "HARRY FROM THE TEENAGE POINT OF VIEW"

Hagrid sends a note saying that Buckbeak has been sentenced to die at sundown. Harry wishes he had the invisibility cloak so they could go see Hagrid, but he left it in the secret passage and cannot let Snape catch him retrieving it. Hermione volunteers to fetch the cloak, and after dinner, the three use it, sneaking out to Hagrid's cottage to comfort him. Hermione, in tears, tries to make tea and discovers Scabbers hiding in a milk jug. Hagrid makes the children leave when they hear men approaching. As they return to the castle, Scabbers squeals, tries to bite Ron, and struggles to get free. They hear the thud of an axe.

Chapter Sixteen

The New Hermione: Over the course of Chapters Fifteen and Sixteen, Hermione undergoes a sort of internal growth spurt. Once a prim tattletale and neurotic student, Hermione shakes off her premature middle age and becomes a daring, mature young adult. She slaps Malfoy and threatens him with her wand, insults a teacher, walks out of a class, and retrieves Harry's invisibility cloak for the purpose of an illicit journey. Rowling suggests that Hermione sees the change in herself and likes it, saying she "look[s] flattered" when Ron remarks on her revolution.

Passive Support: As the characters grow up, their adventures become more serious and their challenges more weighty. As the characters become better equipped to deal with difficult circumstances, Rowling presents them with new problems. In this chapter, Harry, Ron, and Hermione suffer through an execution, knowing they cannot do anything to affect the judicial process. Previously, the three have always found that they can help friends in trouble. Now, for the first time, they must deal with the frustration of powerlessness. The most they can do is visit Hagrid and try to comfort him. This action shows they understand that even when you cannot stop pain, you can comfort those who suffer from it.

CHAPTER SEVENTEEN
Cat, Rat, and Dog

Scabbers continues to squirm and then bites Ron. His skittishness is explained when Harry sees Crookshanks approaching them. Scabbers wriggles loose and runs from Crookshanks. Ron follows him, leaving the invisibility cloak behind. Harry and Hermione run after him. Ron catches Scabbers. A huge dog knocks Harry over, then grabs Ron and drags him into a hidden passage under the Whomping Willow, breaking Ron's leg. Harry and Hermione cannot safely approach the violent Willow until Crookshanks pushes a knot on the tree, making its limbs motionless. They run through the passage and end up inside the Shrieking Shack from Hogsmeade. Ron is inside it with Sirius Black. Ron frantically tells his friends that Black is the dog, too—he is an Animagus, one who can change himself from a man into an animal.

Black takes the children's wands, but Harry attacks him anyway and succeeds in knocking him to the floor and retrieving his own wand. Harry furiously accuses Black of killing his parents. Black replies, "I don't deny it," but says there is a story Harry does not understand. Harry decides to kill Black but cannot make himself do it. Crookshanks jumps in front of Black as if to protect him. Suddenly, Lupin arrives and takes Harry's wand. Lupin seems to come to a realization about Black, saying, "You switched without telling me," and embracing the escaped wizard.

Furious, Hermione says she has been keeping Lupin's secret—he is a werewolf. Lupin admits it, and Harry accuses him of helping Black. Lupin returns the children's wands, hoping this will make them listen to him. He explains that he saw them on the Marauder's Map, which he helped to write under the pseudonym Moody. The map showed Black taking two people into the secret passage. When Ron says it was only him, Lupin asks to see Ron's rat. Lupin informs him that Scabbers is not a rat but an Animagus. He is none other than Peter Pettigrew, the wizard who supposedly died in Black's attack.

UNDERSTANDING AND INTERPRETING
Chapter Seventeen

Motive, Means, Opportunity: When presented with the opportunity to kill Sirius Black, Harry's reaction clarifies his character. Harry believes he has every reason to kill Black, who betrayed the Potters and must take responsibility for their murders at the hands of Voldemort. In addition, Black has been following Harry in the form of a dog, terrifying him, and has just violently accosted Ron, breaking his leg. Moreover, Black is an escaped criminal sought by Muggles and dementors alike. If caught by the authorities, he would likely be tried and killed, so if Harry killed him, he would be expediting the judicial process. Despite all of these sound motives, however, Harry cannot bring himself to kill Black. He has the motives, the means, and the perfect opportunity, but he lacks the ruthlessness of a Dark wizard. He cannot kill in cold blood.

CHAPTER EIGHTEEN
Moony, Wormtail, Padfoot, and Prongs

Black wants to kill Scabbers/Pettigrew immediately, but Lupin says they owe the children an explanation first. Hermione insists that Pettigrew cannot be an Animagus, because he is not in any of the books, but Lupin explains how three Hogwarts students became unregistered Animagi.

PADFOOT ❧ A Yorkshire legend tells of a "nocturnal terror" called the Padfoot. One nineteenth-century book on English folklore calls the Padfoot "about the size of a small donkey, black, with shaggy hair and large eyes like saucers. . . . It follows people by night, or waylays them in the road which they have to pass."

When Lupin was young, a werewolf bit him. Lupin thought his dangerous periods as a wolf made him unfit to attend Hogwarts, but Dumbledore planted the Whomping Willow and built the secret passage and the Shrieking Shack (which was never really haunted) so that Lupin could come to school. When he turned into a wolf each month, he hid in the shack, and the Willow guarded the passage. His three best friends, Sirius Black, Peter Pettigrew, and James Potter, learned to be Animagi so they could safely join him during these exiles. As Animagi, they took to roaming the Hogwarts grounds and eventually made the Marauder's Map. They signed it with their nicknames—Sirius as Padfoot, Peter as Wormtail, and James as Prongs.

Lupin has been trying to decide all year whether to tell Dumbledore that Black is an Animagus. Revealing the secret would mean admitting that he betrayed Dumbledore's trust by cavorting with his Animagi friends when he ought to have been hiding alone in the Shrieking Shack.

Lupin explains that Sirius Black played a trick on Snape, who was always hoping to get the foursome expelled. Black told Snape how to bypass the Whomping Willow, hoping that Snape would encounter Lupin in werewolf form. James Potter stopped Snape, saving him from a deadly encounter with a werewolf. Harry deduces that Snape hates Lupin because he thinks that Lupin was "in on the joke." Suddenly Snape appears, pulling off the invisibility cloak and pointing his wand at Lupin.

UNDERSTANDING AND INTERPRETING
Chapter Eighteen

A Parallel Generation: Rowling borrows well-worn rituals and traditions from other novels, and she creates her own. At Hogwarts, for example, the best students must carry out a ritual struggle among themselves. The current class at Hogwarts plays out conflicts and battles already fought years ago in the Hogwarts class that included Harry's and Malfoy's fathers. When Black describes Snape as someone who was always "sneaking around, trying to find out what we were up to, hoping he could get us expelled," he could be talking about

Draco Malfoy and his attitude toward Harry, Hermione, and Ron. Harry plays his father's role effortlessly, excelling on the Quidditch field and flouting the school rules just as James Potter did.

Dumbledore and Distrust: Now, as years ago, Dumbledore and Hogwarts are steady, calming forces in the lives of the histrionic Hogwarts students. Students have always respected Dumbledore, as we hear from Lupin. Lupin claims he hesitated to reveal Black's Animagus abilities because he did not want Dumbledore to think he had betrayed his trust. Lupin respects Dumbledore in the same way Harry does. Harry and Lupin already have a close friendship, and their shared attitude toward the Headmaster bolsters it. Harry, like Lupin, has felt guilty about betraying Dumbledore's trust by breaking rules at Hogwarts.

CHAPTER NINETEEN
The Servant of Lord Voldemort

Snape has found the Marauder's Map in Lupin's office. Using magic, he ties up Lupin and announces that he will deliver him and Black to the dementors. Hermione asks Snape to listen to Lupin and Black, but Snape calls her a "stupid girl." Harry blocks Snape's way, saying that a schoolboy grudge is making him act pathetically. Snape orders him out of the way, but Harry disarms him. Snape slams into the wall and gets knocked unconscious; Harry turns and sees that Hermione and Ron performed the disarming spell at the same time he did.

Ron asks Black how he can be sure that Scabbers, of all the rats in the world, is Pettigrew. Black shows him the photo of the Weasley family from the *Daily Prophet*. Scabbers, who sits on Ron's shoulder in the photo, is missing a toe. Black explains that when he cornered Pettigrew on the street, Peter yelled out that Black had betrayed the Potters. He then cut off his own finger, blew apart the street, turned into a rat, and disappeared into the sewer. Black explains how Crookshanks has helped him by trying to catch Scabbers/Pettigrew (who once again faked his own death) and by stealing the password from Neville. Lupin tells Harry that all this time he thought Black had betrayed the Potters, but really it was Pettigrew. Harry yells that Black admitted killing his parents. Black explains he feels responsible for their deaths because he convinced Lily and James to use Peter instead of him as the Secret-Keeper.

Lupin and Black force Scabbers to transform into the sniveling figure of Peter Pettigrew. As Pettigrew squeaks in terror and Black rages in anger, the true story of the Potters' death emerges. Black suggested Pettigrew for the Secret-Keeper to throw Voldemort off the scent, thinking Voldemort would never suspect a "weak, talentless" wizard like Pettigrew. But Pettigrew was already a spy for Voldemort. Since the Potters' deaths, he has been hiding, afraid that Voldemort's remaining supporters will blame him for Voldemort's downfall at Harry's hands. Pettigrew found his way to the Weasleys, hoping to hear news of Voldemort's resurgence.

Lupin and Black prepare to kill Pettigrew, who begs Ron, Hermione, and Harry to intercede. Finally Harry asks for mercy. He says that James Potter would not have wanted his friends to become killers. He suggests they give Pettigrew to the dementors. Lupin uses his wand to bind Pettigrew, put bandages on Ron's broken leg, and levitate Snape's limp body. Black chains Pettigrew to Lupin and Ron, and they all leave the room.

UNDERSTANDING AND INTERPRETING
Chapter Nineteen

An Unexpected Conclusion: In Chapter Nineteen, Rowling ties up many loose ends and leaves others dangling. It is now clear that the wrongful conviction of Crookshanks for Scabbers's death parallels the events of twelve years ago, when Sirius Black was wrongfully convicted for Pettigrew's death. Some assumptions that seemed silly are proved right. For example, Ron always insisted that Crookshanks hated Scabbers, an insistence that seemed strange. Now we learn that Crookshanks had good reason to hate the murderer-in-hiding. Some assumptions that seemed reasonable are proved wrong. For instance, we assumed that Sirius Black was a psychopathic murderer bent on killing Harry. Now we learn that he stalked Hogwarts to find Pettigrew, not Harry. In her usual fashion, Rowling makes this chapter of explanation a surprising one, drawing together the small clues sprinkled through previous chapters to make an unexpected conclusion.

The Precipitating Event: Most novels begin with a major event that sets the plot in motion. We often recognize this event right away, but in *Harry Potter and the Prisoner of Azkaban*, Rowling buries the precipitating event in a flurry of other details. The event comes in the first chapter of the novel, when Harry receives a number of birthday presents and notes, among them a newspaper clipping from Ron featuring a picture of the Weasleys in Egypt. The publication of that photograph, innocuous as it seemed at first mention, was the moment that set in motion the events of the novel, prompting Black to escape from prison and set off in search of Pettigrew.

CHAPTER TWENTY

The Dementor's Kiss

Black says that the Potters appointed him as Harry's guardian, and Harry can come and live with him once his name is cleared. This news thrills Harry. The group arrives back on Hogwarts grounds and heads toward the castle. Then the moon comes out from behind a cloud, and Lupin starts to turn into a wolf. Black tells Harry to run, then turns into a dog and begins to drag Lupin away. Pettigrew picks up Lupin's wand and knocks out Ron and Crookshanks. Harry disarms him, but Pettigrew has already transformed into Scabbers. He flees. Lupin, now a werewolf, runs away, and Black, in dog form, chases Scabbers.

Harry and Hermione hear the sound of a dog in pain and run to help Black. By the shore of the lake, they see Black, now in human form, surrounded by dementors. Harry tries to conjure a Patronus by thinking of his future life with Black. Hermione, exhausted, drops to the ground. One of the dementors takes off his hood, and Harry sees its mouth, a gaping hole. The dementor sweeps aside Harry's Patronus and grabs Harry by the throat, preparing to kiss him. Harry begins to feel cold and miserable, but suddenly he finds himself released. A bright light in the shape of an animal chases off the dementors. On the far shore of the lake, Harry sees a familiar figure petting the animal. Harry faints.

UNDERSTANDING AND INTERPRETING
Chapter Twenty

Twists and Turns: This chapter, which moves more quickly than any other part of the story, is also the shortest chapter of the novel. First, Harry finds a thrilling prospect for the future when Sirius Black, an adult he realizes he likes and respects, offers him a home. Harry can escape the Dursleys and live with someone who loved the Potters, as the Dursleys do not, and understands wizardry, which the Dursleys cannot. Forced to use his strongest happy thought to conjure a Patronus, Harry thinks of Black, an indication that the newfound love of a trustworthy adult makes Harry happier than anything in his life has made him before. Happily for all wizards, a servant of Voldemort has been unmasked and captured. However, in the space of three pages, the neatly sewn-up ending seems to unravel completely. Pettigrew escapes, the recently mended Ron is injured again, and dementors close in on Black and Harry. The happy ending has been wrenched away. Then, three pages later, the plot twists again. Harry has been saved from the dementor by a figure that could be his father.

HOGWARTS IN SCOTLAND

Hogwarts is several hours north of London by train, and Rowling has said that the school is in northern Scotland, wellspring of Celtic lore and legend. As the term nears its end, Harry and his friends enjoy long northern days. In this chapter, the sky stays light well into the evening.

Don

Athol

Forfar

Perth

Dundee

Arbr

Tay Mouth

St And

Cupar

C. Fi

Forth Ba

Clackmann

Dun

Leith

Hurle

EDINBURGH

Green

Fal

J. K. Rowling

CHAPTER TWENTY-ONE
Hermione's Secret

Harry awakens in the hospital ward to hear Snape boasting that he heroically saved the three students from a werewolf and Sirius Black. Cornelius Fudge promises Snape an award for his courage. Ron is still unconscious, but Harry and Hermione leap out of bed and begin explaining what they saw and heard, talking about Pettigrew's appearance and Black's innocence. Snape waves away their explanations, saying that Black must have confounded their minds. Harry and Hermione are still heatedly defending Black when Dumbledore enters the room and says he must speak with the two of them alone. Once the others have left, Dumbledore tells Harry and Hermione that he has heard Black's story and he believes it, but not one shred of evidence exists to back it up. The dementors are on their way to Sirius Black, who is locked in Flitwick's office. Dumbledore looks at Hermione and pointedly remarks that they need more time if they are going to save two innocent lives.

Hermione, taking the hint, brings out a small hourglass which McGonagall gave her so she could attend all of her classes. Hermione uses the hourglass to take herself and Harry three hours back in time. They must avoid being seen at all costs, since a major wizarding law forbids tampering with time. Harry realizes that Dumbledore wants them to free Buckbeak, who can fly up to Flitwick's office and rescue Black. They creep out to Hagrid's cottage along the edge of the forest and wait until they see themselves leave and Macnair look out the window at Buckbeak. While Fudge reads the notice of execution, Harry unties Buckbeak and drags him into the woods. Harry, Hermione, and Buckbeak hide in the forest as they hear the thud of an axe swung in frustration at having lost the victim, as well as Hagrid's howl of joy at the surprise escape. They wait in the woods, watching themselves go down the Whomping Willow and emerge from it again.

While Hermione and Buckbeak hide from the werewolf in Hagrid's empty cabin, Harry cannot resist slipping out to see if it was really his father who conjured the Patronus. He watches the dementors approach and attempt to kiss him. Nothing happens. No Patronus comes to save Harry. Suddenly, Harry realizes that it was he who conjured the powerful Patronus, not his father. The familiar figure he saw was his future self—the self he is now—standing across the lake. Harry conjures the huge animal he saw before, saving his, Hermione's, and Black's life. When the animal returns, Harry finally realizes that the Patronus is a stag, Prongs, his father's Animagus form. Father and son regard each other, and then the father disappears.

154

Harry and Hermione fly Buckbeak to Flitwick's window, which Hermione opens with her wand. Black joins them on Buckbeak. The hippogriff lands on the battlements, and the children get off. Before he leaves, Black tells Harry he is truly his father's son. Then he flies away on Buckbeak.

UNDERSTANDING AND INTERPRETING
Chapter Twenty-One

Self-Reliance: It strikes Hermione as odd that Harry can suddenly perform the advanced magic that eluded him before, conjuring a Patronus capable of vanquishing the dementors. Harry explains, "I knew I could do it this time . . . because I'd already done it." Magic is a mental activity, not a physical one, and all Harry needed in order to conjure the Patronus, aside from Lupin's rigorous training, was a firm belief in his ability to do so. The interaction between the two Harrys, James Potter, and the Patronus shows how thoroughly Harry's father pervades Harry's consciousness. When Harry saw his future self across the lake, he mistook the figure for his father. When he finally succeeds in conjuring a strong Patronus, he conjures his father in animal form. Even if the stag is not James, but Harry's wish made flesh, the ghostly presence comforts Harry. James Potter is dead, but Harry still wants to rely on him for protection. Actually, as we see when Harry mistakes himself for his father, the person Harry relies on is himself.

Tidy Storytelling: Satisfying endings are Rowling's trademark. She gathers together even the most peripheral threads of the story, binding them into a pleasing whole. In Chapter Twenty-One, we learn that Hermione has been taking classes and exams simultaneously by using a magical Time-Turner. Her overbooked schedule, which once seemed like a small detail, becomes centrally important when she uses the Time-Turner to save Sirius Black. Harry's antidementor lessons, which originally seemed like a relatively unimportant way to succeed in sports, end up saving three lives. Finally, a passing reference to James Potter as "Prongs" takes on new significance when Harry calls out to his father using that name.

THE NEW YORK TIMES
BESTSELLER LIST

In July 2000, around the time the fourth Harry Potter novel was published, the *New York Times* created a new bestseller list for children's books. The first three volumes of the Harry Potter series, which had topped the fiction list for over a year, were moved to this new list. Some children's book publishers were happy about the free publicity generated by the new list. Some critics claimed that Harry had been unjustly banished from the more prestigious fiction list.

birth both decide to run the a
— but without knowing they are related.

15* **FINAL JUSTICE,** by W. E. B. Griffin. (Putnam, $26.95.) A detective in the Philadelphia Police Department is caught up in three murder investigations; eighth volume in the "Badge of Honor" series.

CHILDREN'S PAPERBACK

1 **HARRY POTTER AND THE GOBLET OF FIRE,** by Rowling. (Scholastic, $8.99.) A British boy takes p a series of contests against other aspiring wizard (Ages 10 and up)

2 **HARRY POTTER AND THE PRISONER OF AZI BAN,** by J. K. Rowling. (Scholastic, $7.99.) A boy at witchcraft school is threatened. (Ages 10 and

3 **HARRY POTTER AND THE CHAMBER OF SE CRETS,** by J. K. Rowling. (Scholastic, $6.99.) returns to witchcraft school. (Ages 10 and up)

EASTER BASKET, adapted by Sarah

CHAPTER TWENTY-TWO
Owl Post Again

Harry and Hermione sneak back to the hospital wing, arriving as Dumbledore is about to lock the door. Harry tells him of their success. When the other Harry and Hermione, the ones in the hospital, have gone back in time, the returning Harry and Hermione slip back into their beds.

Snape, livid at Black's escape, insists that Harry had something to do with it. Dumbledore says that Harry has been locked in the hospital. Fudge removes the dementors, expressing shock that they tried to kiss an innocent student.

The next day, Harry, Ron, and Hermione go to see Hagrid, who is happy about Buckbeak's escape. Hagrid says that Snape told the Slytherins that Lupin is a werewolf, a revelation that caused Lupin to resign. Harry goes to see Lupin, who explains that Snape's news will upset the students' parents. He says he is proud of how much Harry has learned. He gives Harry the invisibility cloak and the Marauder's Map.

> "J.K. Rowling is a literary artist, and these three books possess more imaginative life than the majority of novels that are published in this country in any given year. They are full of marvelous invention and humor and fun, but they have more than that. . . . With Harry Potter, Rowling has brought reality back into the literature of escape."
>
> **LEE SIEGEL**, *THE NEW REPUBLIC*

Dumbledore arrives, and Lupin leaves. Harry is angry and upset that Pettigrew got away. He tells Dumbledore how Trelawney went into a trance and predicted a servant of Voldemort's would return to his master and help make him powerful again. Dumbledore, surprised, says this marks the second time that Trelawney has made a real prediction. He says Harry did right to save Pettigrew, and that James Potter would have done the same. Pettigrew may have escaped, but Harry has sent Voldemort a servant who owes his life to Harry, a good wizard. When one wizard saves another, Dumbledore says, a bond is created between them. Of the Patronus, Dumbledore says, "Your father is alive in you."

Harry, Ron, and Hermione pass their exams. Gryffindor wins the House Championship. Hermione drops Muggle studies and decides to have a normal schedule next year, one that does not involve time travel. Harry is depressed that he lost his chance to escape the Dursleys and live with his godfather. On the Hogwarts Express, Harry receives a letter from Sirius Black delivered by a tiny owl. Black, who is safe in hiding, admits to sending Harry the Firebolt and writes, "If you ever need me, send word." He includes a note giving Harry permission to visit Hogsmeade and offers the owl to Ron, to replace Scabbers.

At the station, Harry tells Mr. Dursley that his godfather is a convicted murderer who likes to check in on him and make sure he is happy.

UNDERSTANDING AND INTERPRETING
Chapter Twenty-Two

Debriefing Dumbledore: As he has at the end of the previous two novels, Harry has an important talk with Dumbledore in this final chapter. Dumbledore tells Harry, "The consequences of our actions are always so complicated, so diverse, that predicting the future is a very difficult business indeed." His words might serve as a challenge to readers who want to guess what will happen in future novels in the series. They also encourage Harry to take a mature view of his actions instead of thinking of them as either good or bad. Harry spared the life of Voldemort's servant, perhaps even indirectly precipitating Voldemort's rise to power, but there is no way to immediately judge the consequences of his mercy.

Dark Tone: Although *Harry Potter and the Prisoner of Azkaban* ends tidily, with mysteries explained and loose ends tied up, a dark tone, absent from the first two novels, pervades the resolution. Justice was done, but only to a certain extent: Sirius Black is still unfairly considered dangerous and must hide from the authorities, Pettigrew is on the loose again, and Harry must worry about the accidental aid he gave Voldemort. The ambiguous conclusion befits Harry, Hermione, and Ron, who are growing up and beginning to understand the moral complexities of the world.

Conclusions

In his book *Sticks and Stones,* Jack Zipes writes, "The phenomenal aspect of the reception of the Harry Potter books has blurred the focus for anyone who wants to take literature for young people seriously." It can be difficult to separate the true literary value of the Harry Potter books from the astonishing commercial hype that has accompanied their publication. "Pottermania" has become more frenzied with the publication of each new novel in the series. By the time Rowling released the fourth volume, readers were standing in long lines to buy the book at midnight on publication day. Harry Potter merchandise of every sort abounds, from towels to jewelry boxes to vibrating brooms. The first two Harry Potter films opened to lukewarm reviews, further muddying the actual merit of the novels.

Those baffled or annoyed by the storm of money and publicity accompanying the Potter phenomenon should turn away from the hype and toward the novels. Reading the Harry Potter series reveals allusions to folklore, history, mythology, and popular culture, as well as nuances of character, description, and dialogue—none of which the films can cover in full. Reading the novels with an awareness of Lewis Carroll, C. S. Lewis, J.R.R. Tolkien, Thomas Hughes, and Roald Dahl, files them where they belong—in the canon of fantasy novels.

SUGGESTIONS
FOR FURTHER
READING

Acocella, Joan. "Under the Spell: Harry Potter Explained." *The New Yorker* (31 July 2000), 74–78.

Colbert, David. *The Magical Worlds of Harry Potter: A Treasury of Myths, Legends, Facts, and Fascinating Facts*. Wrightsville Beach, NC: Lumina Press, 2001.

Gray, Paul. "Wild About Harry." *Time* (20 September 1999), 66–72.

Heilman, Elizabeth. *Harry Potter's World: Multidisciplinary Critical Perspectives*. New York: Routledge, 2002.

Hunt, Peter. *Children's Literature*. Oxford: Blackwell, 2001.

Iyer, Pico. "The Playing Fields of Hogwarts." *New York Times* 19 October 1999.

Kronzek, Allan Zola and Elizabeth Kronzek. *The Sorcerer's Companion: A Guide to the Magical World of Harry Potter.* New York: Broadway Books, 2001.

Natov, Roni. "Harry Potter and the Extraordinariness of the Ordinary." *The Lion and the Unicorn*, vol. 25, no. 2 (April 2001), 310–327.

Neal, Connie. *What's a Christian to Do with Harry Potter?* Colorado Springs: Waterbrook Press, 2001.

Pennington, John. "From Elfland to Hogwarts, or the Aesthetic Trouble with Harry Potter." *The Lion and the Unicorn*, vol. 26, no. 1 (Jan. 2002), 78–97.

Radoch, Daniel. "Why American Kids Don't Consider Harry Potter an Insufferable Prig." *New Yorker* (20 Sept. 1999), 54–55.

Schafer, Elizabeth D. *Exploring Harry Potter: Beacham's Sourcebook for Teaching Young Adult Fiction*. Osprey, FL: Beacham Publishing Corp., 2000.

Shapiro, Marc. *J.K. Rowling: The Wizard Behind Harry Potter*. New York: St. Martin's Griffin, 2001.

Siegel, Lee. "Harry Potter and the Spirit of the Age: Fear of Flying." *New Republic* (22 November 1999), 40–44.

Stuttaford, Andrew. "It's Witchcraft." *National Review* (11 Oct. 1999), 60–62.

Zipes, Jack. *Sticks and Stones: The Troublesome Success of Children's Literature from Slovenly Peter to Harry Potter.* New York & London: Routledge, 2001.

INDEX

D

Dahl, Roald 7, 57, 159
Daily Prophet 25, 78, 79, 120, 149
Dark Arts 55, 64, 78, 92, 94
David Copperfield 6
Davies 113
death 51, 57, 86, 115, 117, 123, 126, 129
Defense Against the Dark Arts 16, 27, 63, 67, 78, 83, 115, 127, 132, 133
Delaney-Podmore, Sir Patrick 65, 68
dementors 112, 113, 115, 127–128, 134–135, 136–140, 151
Derek 113
Derrick 113
detective novels 6
Devil's Snare 53
Diagon Alley 15, 25–28, 66, 77, 114, 123
Dickens, Charles 6, 7
Diggle, Dedalus 13
Diggory, Cedric 113, 134
Professor Dippet 95
Dippet, Armando 65
Divination 129–130, 142–145
Dobby 65, 73–75, 89, 91, 107, 123
Dumbledore, Albus (Headmaster of Hogwarts) 12, 13, 14, 19, 27, 29, 39, 53, 57–59, 65, 68, 69, 79, 87, 89, 92–94, 97, 102–107, 108, 114, 133–134, 149, 154, 157–158
Dursley, Dudley 13, 14, 16, 20, 58, 65, 71, 114, 119
Dursley, Petunia 13, 18, 23–24, 65, 75, 114, 119
Dursley, Vernon 13, 18–24, 25, 65, 71–76, 114, 116, 119, 121

E

Eager, Edward 112

Ebert, Roger 56
Eeylops Owl Emporium 15
Emma 6
England 3, 11, 63, 74, 111
Errol 65, 77, 114, 119
Eton 41
Exeter University 3
exile 59

F

fairy tales 6, 59
fame 30, 31, 34, 78, 81–84, 92, 108
Famous Five, The 72
Fang 14, 34, 50, 65, 97, 98, 114
Fantastic Beasts and Where to Find Them 54
fantasy 11, 12, 63, 159
Fat Friar, the 14, 66
Fat Lady, the 14, 31, 113, 114, 132–134
Fawkes 66, 102
Mrs. Figg 14, 20
Filch, Argus 12, 14, 15, 35, 38, 42, 49, 50, 66, 68, 84–87, 114, 118, 135, 141
Finch-Fletchley, Justin 66, 83, 87, 92
Finnigan, Seamus 14, 34, 66, 114, 131
Firenze 14, 50–51
Flamel, Nicolas 14, 29, 39, 42–46, 126
Flint, Marcus 14, 66, 84, 114
Professor Flitwick (Charms) 14, 36, 48, 66, 114, 136, 154–155
Floo Powder 77
Flourish and Blotts 77–78, 105
Fluffy 14, 35–36, 39, 48, 53
folklore 74, 100, 131, 148, 152, 159
Forbidden Forest 13, 14, 16, 31, 45, 50–51
Fortescue, Florean 114

Index

Index

SPARKNOTES™ LITERATURE GUIDES

1984

The Adventures of
  Huckleberry Finn

The Adventures of Tom
  Sawyer

The Aeneid

All Quiet on the Western
  Front

And Then There Were
  None

Angela's Ashes

Animal Farm

Anna Karenina

Anne of Green Gables

Anthem

Antony and Cleopatra

Aristotle's Ethics

As I Lay Dying

As You Like It

Atlas Shrugged

The Autobiography of
  Malcolm X

The Awakening

The Bean Trees

The Bell Jar

Beloved

Beowulf

Billy Budd

Black Boy

Bless Me, Ultima

The Bluest Eye

Brave New World

The Brothers Karamazov

The Call of the Wild

Candide

The Canterbury Tales

Catch-22

The Catcher in the Rye

The Chocolate War

The Chosen

Cold Mountain

Cold Sassy Tree

The Color Purple

The Count of Monte
  Cristo

Crime and Punishment

The Crucible

Cry, the Beloved Country

Cyrano de Bergerac

David Copperfield

Death of a Salesman

The Death of Socrates

The Diary of a Young Girl

A Doll's House

Don Quixote

Dr. Faustus

Dr. Jekyll and Mr. Hyde

Dracula

Dune

Edith Hamilton's
  Mythology

Emma

Ethan Frome

Fahrenheit 451

Fallen Angels

A Farewell to Arms

Farewell to Manzanar

Flowers for Algernon

For Whom the Bell Tolls

The Fountainhead

Frankenstein

The Giver

The Glass Menagerie

Gone With the Wind

The Good Earth

The Grapes of Wrath

Great Expectations

The Great Gatsby

Grendel

Gulliver's Travels

Hamlet

The Handmaid's Tale

Hard Times

Harry Potter and the
  Sorcerer's Stone

Heart of Darkness

Henry IV, Part I

Henry V

Hiroshima

The Hobbit

The House of Seven
  Gables

I Know Why the Caged
  Bird Sings

The Iliad

Inferno

Inherit the Wind

Invisible Man

Jane Eyre

Johnny Tremain

The Joy Luck Club

Julius Caesar

The Jungle

The Killer Angels

King Lear

The Last of the Mohicans

Les Miserables

A Lesson Before Dying

The Little Prince

Little Women

Lord of the Flies

The Lord of the Rings

Macbeth

Madame Bovary

A Man for All Seasons

The Mayor of
  Casterbridge

The Merchant of Venice

A Midsummer Night's
  Dream

Moby Dick

Much Ado About Nothing

My Antonia

Narrative of the Life of
  Frederick Douglass

Native Son

The New Testament

Night

Notes from Underground

The Odyssey

The Oedipus Plays

Of Mice and Men

The Old Man and the Sea

The Old Testament

Oliver Twist

The Once and Future
  King

One Day in the Life of
  Ivan Denisovich

One Flew Over the
  Cuckoo's Nest

One Hundred Years of
  Solitude

Othello

Our Town

The Outsiders

Paradise Lost

A Passage to India

The Pearl

The Picture of Dorian
  Gray

Poe's Short Stories

A Portrait of the Artist as
  a Young Man

Pride and Prejudice

The Prince

A Raisin in the Sun

The Red Badge of
  Courage

The Republic

Richard III

Robinson Crusoe

Romeo and Juliet

The Scarlet Letter

A Separate Peace

Silas Marner

Sir Gawain

Slaughterhouse-Five

Snow Falling on Cedars

Song of Solomon

The Sound and the Fury

Steppenwolf

The Stranger

Streetcar Named Desire

The Sun Also Rises

A Tale of Two Cities

The Taming of the Shrew

The Tempest

Tess of the d'Ubervilles

The Things They Carried

Their Eyes Were
  Watching God

Things Fall Apart

To Kill a Mockingbird

To the Lighthouse

Treasure Island

Twelfth Night

Ulysses

Uncle Tom's Cabin

Walden

War and Peace

Wuthering Heights

A Yellow Raft in Blue
  Water